# THE
# BAKERS'
# MANUAL

# THE
# BAKERS'
# MANUAL

## FOURTH EDITION

# JOSEPH AMENDOLA

 VAN NOSTRAND REINHOLD
————————————New York

Library of Congress Catalog Card Number   92–22690
ISBN 0-442-00997-6

Printed in the United States of America.

Van Nostrand Reinhold
115 Fifth Avenue
New York, New York 10003

Chapman and Hall
2-6 Boundary Row
London, SE1 8HN, England

Thomas Nelson Australia
102 Dodds Street
South Melbourne 3205
Victoria, Australia

Nelson Canada
1120 Birchmount Road
Scarborough, Ontario MIK 5G4, Canada

16  15  14  13  12  11  10  9  8  7  6  5  4  3  2  1

Library of Congress Cataloging-in-Publication Data

Amendola, Joseph.
  The bakers' manual/Joseph Amendola.—4th ed.
     p.    cm.
  Previous eds. published as: The baker's manual for quantity baking and pastry making.
  Includes index.
  ISBN 0-442-00997-6
  1. Baking.  2. Cake.  3. Pastry.  4. Desserts.  I. Amendola, Joseph. The baker's manual for quantity baking and pastry making.
  II. Title
  TX763.A27    1992
  641.8'65—dc20                                                            92–22690
                                                                               CIP

*This book is dedicated to my wife,*
*Marjorie D. Amendola*

*As Brillat-Savarin so aptly put it, "The discovery of a new dish is more important to the happiness of mankind than the discovery of a new star."*

# CONTENTS

# PREFACE

This fourth revision is intended to combine new recipes with the old, now being brought up-to-date.

At this time I would like to acknowledge the help and support given freely by friends and colleagues as well as by the many graduates who have helped in my happy and interesting career.

Since the 1940s, I have been associated with the Culinary Institute of America in various capacities: Vice President of Faculty, Dean of Students and Vice President of Student Affairs, and Acting President of Administration.

I have traveled extensively as a food and hospitality consultant for major food companies; baking and desserts have been my specialty. I now live in Orlando, Florida, and am involved as a partner with Fessel International as a consultant in baking.

JOSEPH AMENDOLA

# CHAPTER ONE

# INGREDIENTS

## FLOUR

Flour is the finely ground meal of wheat and is one of the most important ingredients used in bakery products. Therefore, flour quality has a major influence on the quality of the finished baked products. It is important for the following reasons:

1. It is the backbone and structure of baked goods.
2. It acts as a binding agent and an absorbing agent.
3. It affects the keeping quality of products.
4. It is important to the flavor of products.
5. It adds nutritional value to the baked product.

### Wheat

Wheat, from which flour is made, is the most essential grain used in bread-making because it is the only cereal that contains the proper combination of glutenin and gliadin. When flour is combined with water, these properties form gluten, essential for retaining the gas produced by yeast. No other grain can replace wheat in bread-making.

The primary types of wheat flour used in baking are hard wheat and soft wheat.

**Hard wheat** contains a high proportion of gluten, which makes it an excellent choice for breads and breadstuffs. There are several kinds of hard wheat:

1. *One hundred percent straight flour,* a strong flour, is preferred in the production of high-quality hard rolls and hearth breads. Here it produces the best results.
2. *Patent flour,* generally employed when a formula calls for bread flour, is used in making bread, rolls, and products commonly made with bread flour.
3. *First clear flour* and *second clear flour* are used in making rye breads because of their darker color and higher gluten content.
4. *Bran* is used mainly in the production of muffins.
5. *Whole wheat flour* (including *graham*) is used primarily in making whole wheat bread and muffins.

**Soft wheat** generally contains less gluten than hard wheat and is commonly used for making the more delicate baked goods. There are three kinds of soft wheat: *cake flour,* which is used to produce high-quality cakes, and *pastry flour* and *cookie flour,* which are used for piecrusts, cookies, and pastries.

## Rye Flour

Rye flour is milled from rye grain. The composition is similar to that of wheat, but the protein or gluten components are quite different.

The protein of rye flour, when made into dough with the addition of water, does not produce gluten as hard wheat does if treated the same way. It is necessary to use some hard wheat flour, such as first or second clear, with rye flour to obtain a porous, well-raised loaf. If rye flour alone is used, the finished product is heavy, somewhat soggy, hard to digest, and unpalatable.

Rye is milled into rye meal or pumpernickel, patent or light rye flour, medium or rye flour, and dark rye flour.

**Rye blend** is prepared in the mills by mixing a proportion of rye flour with high gluten or clear flour. The proportion of the blend is usually 25 to 40 percent of rye flour to clear flour. The exact amount used depends on local demand and the type of loaf desired. Therefore, the baker must be the judge as to the proper proportions of the blend to be used.

Points of interest concerning the making of rye bread are as follows:

1. Depending on the type of rye bread desired, the formula must be adjusted. A higher proportion of dark rye flour must be adjusted. A higher proportion of dark rye flour must be used for a heavy dark rye loaf.
2. Rye dough should not be mixed for as long a period as dough for light breads.

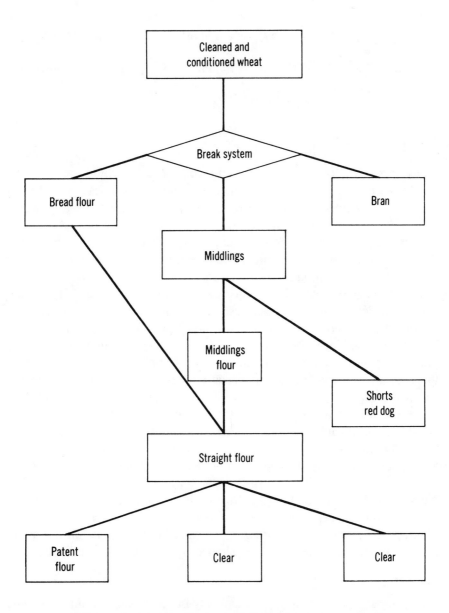

The above diagram shows the general separation of the various grades of flour, but does not show the exact system of the separation of flour streams.

This chart is reprinted from a **Treatise on Cake Making** by permission of Standard Brands, Inc., copyright owner.

*Figure 1.1   The milling of wheat into flour*

3. Rye dough should always have a short period of fermentation for the best results.

4. In baking rye bread, steam is required in the oven during the first ten minutes of the baking period.

## EGGS

When "eggs" are listed, *whole eggs*—the yolks and the whites—are meant.

Eggs are natural emulsifying agents and so help to produce a smooth batter. This batter may be satisfactorily aerated by creaming or beating, which retains the gases produced by leavening agents.

Heat coagulates eggs at approximately 126°F. This is an important characteristic because such thickening permits eggs to form part of the framework and structure of the product being baked.

Because egg yolks contain fat, they have a shortening action. This is particularly noticeable when eggs are used in sponge cakes and yeast products.

Insofar as leavening action is concerned, egg whites perform the same function as whole eggs. In angel food cake, for example, whipped egg whites produce a foamy mass made of minute air cells that expand when they reach the heat of the oven. Because the egg whites are able to hold air in the batter, the batter increases in volume, and when the heat of the oven hits it, the eggs coagulate and form part of the cell structure of the cake.

Eggs are important because they add color, improve the grain and texture of baked products, increase volume, give structure to the product, add flavor, and have considerable nutritional value. Egg whites figure largely in some of the above points as they are responsible for increasing volume, improving the grain and texture, and giving structure to the product.

There are two types of eggs used in bakeries: shelled eggs and frozen eggs. With few exceptions, both types give the same results in the finished products. In those exceptions, however, shelled eggs produce better results.

### Shelled Eggs

Quality eggs must be used to ensure quality in the finished products. Shelled eggs may be converted into weight as follows:

9 to 11 shelled eggs = 1 lb of whole eggs
15 to 17 shelled egg whites = 1 lb of egg whites
22 to 24 shelled egg yolks = 1 lb of egg yolks

## Frozen Eggs

Frozen eggs have the following advantages:

1. They save time and labor because breaking and separating are not necessary.
2. They avoid waste through spoilage and other causes.
3. An adequate supply of uniform quality is assured, and uniform quality means better results.

Frozen eggs are sold as whole eggs, yolks, whites, or specials, which contain whole eggs and extra yolks.

## SALT

The following are the most important functions performed by salt in baked products:

1. It brings out the desired flavor.
2. It controls yeast action. Increasing the salt content slows the yeast action but assists in preventing the development of objectionable bacteria and the wild types of yeast that are harmful to the dough.
3. It has a strengthening effect on the gluten in flour. It also helps the dough hold carbon dioxide gas more effectively.
4. It improves the texture and grain of baked products.

## MILK

Many different forms of milk are used in the bakery. Following is a list of the types, their origin, or the method of their production:

1. *Liquid whole milk* is milk in its natural form as it comes from the cow.
2. *Liquid skim milk* is produced by removing the butterfat from whole milk.
3. *Buttermilk* is the product that remains after the butterfat has been extracted from the separated cream.
4. *Sweetened condensed whole milk* is made by adding sugar to whole milk, then condensing it (that is, partially evaporating the water from it) until it reaches the required consistency.

5. *Powdered whole and skim milk* is produced in two ways. In the first method, the milk is condensed until a considerable amount of water has been removed. It is then forced through a small opening into a heated chamber where most of the remaining water is removed so that the milk contains only 2½ to 4 percent of moisture. In the second method, the milk is forced through an opening into a heated chamber in which air is being circulated. By this method, the moisture is removed after it leaves the spray.

To reconstitute dry milk powder, water should be added in the following proportions:

*Liquid whole milk:* 12½ percent solids; 87½ percent water
*Liquid skim milk:* 9 percent solids; 91 percent water

To reconstitute whole milk powder into 1 lb of liquid milk:

$16 \times 12\frac{1}{2}\% = 2$ oz of whole milk powder
$16 \times 87\frac{1}{2}\% = 14$ oz of water
Total                16 oz of whole milk

To reconstitute skim milk powder into 1 lb of liquid skim milk:

$16 \times 9\% = 1.44$ oz of skim milk powder
$16 \times 91\% = 14.56$ oz of water
Total                16 oz of skim milk

In bakery products, milk improves the texture, food value, keeping quality, and flavor.

## SWEETENING AGENTS

### Sugar

Cane sugar and beet sugar are both sucrose (sugar) obtained from sugarcane and sugar beets. If refined to the same degree, there is no difference in the sugar whether derived from cane or beets.

Sugar may be secured in the following forms:

1. *Granulated sugar*—the ordinary standard sugar.
2. *Fine granulated sugar,* sometimes called *berry* or *fruit sugar,* is the

preferred type of sugar for cake baking. There are several grades known as fine, extra fine, etc.

3. *Confectioners' sugar* (also called *powdered sugar).*
4. *Pulverized sugar,* usually known as *icing sugar,* sometimes contains a small amount of starch to prevent lumping.
5. *Brown sugar,* which contains 85 to 92% sucrose, is used primarily for flavor.

## Honey

Honey is a natural invert syrup produced from the nectar of flowers by the honeybee. It varies in composition, depending upon its source. Clover honey is considered one of the best for bakery use because flavor is its primary function.

An average sample of honey contains about 75% invert sugar, 15 to 20% moisture, and a small amount of other substances, which give it the delicious flavor.

All lots of honey should be tasted upon delivery to check flavor qualities.

## Molasses

Molasses is secured by concentrating the juice of the sugar cane. It contains 35 to 50% sucrose, 20 to 25% water, and the balance of invert sugar, mineral matter, small amounts of protein, and other substances.

Molasses should be checked for flavor before use.

## YEAST

Yeast is a microscopic plant or cell grown in vats containing a warm mash of ground corn, barley malt, and water. The two types of yeast are compressed yeast and dry yeast.

If dry yeast is to be replaced by compressed yeast in a formula, approximately 40% of dry yeast by weight is used. For example, if a formula calls for 1 lb of compressed yeast and this must be replaced by dry yeast, 40% of 1 lb, or 6.5 oz of dry yeast, is used. The remaining 60%, or 9.5 oz, is water.

Following are the various reactions of yeast to different temperatures:

| | |
|---|---|
| 60°–70°F | Slow reaction |
| 80°F | Normal reaction |
| 90°–100°F | Fast reaction |
| 138°F | Terminal death point |

The ideal storing temperature for yeast is 30° to 45°F.

When yeast is mixed with flour into a dough, the yeast plants begin to grow and multiply very fast. This growth produces the leavening gas, or carbon dioxide, which forms the small bubbles that cause the dough to rise.

Yeast in baked products increases the volume and improves the grain, the texture, and the flavor.

## CHEMICAL LEAVENERS

Chemical leaveners may be divided into two classes: acids, such as bicarbonate of soda or baking powder, and ammonium carbonate.

1. **Acid leaveners.** In the case of baking powder, an acid-reacting salt or a combination of such salts acts upon sodium bicarbonate in the presence of moisture and heat, releasing carbon dioxide gas, which leavens the product. Sodium bicarbonate contains carbon and oxygen, which form carbon dioxide gas. Hence, the reaction is similar whether a baking powder is used containing both the acid component and the sodium bicarbonate, or whether the sodium bicarbonate is added to a batter that has sufficient acidity in other ingredients to release the gas from the sodium bicarbonate.

   An example of this is the addition of sodium bicarbonate to spice cakes containing molasses. The molasses is acid and is able to release the carbon dioxide gas from the added sodium bicarbonate.

2. **Ammonium carbonate** is a little different in its action. Like sodium bicarbonate, it also contains the constituents of carbon dioxide gas. Unlike the acid type, however, it does not require an acid or other substance to cause a reaction. Carbon dioxide gas is liberated from the ammonium carbonate by decomposition due to heat and moisture in the baking process. Because it decomposes rapidly, it is used primarily in cream puffs and cookies, where a sudden expansion is desirable.

Chemical leaveners used in baked products improve their grain and texture; they bring about more uniform symmetry and increase volume.

## FATS AND SHORTENINGS

Fats used for baking purposes are all edible fats or hydrogenated oils of vegetable or animal origin such as hydrogenated shortening, lard oils, butter, and oleomargarine.

*Oleomargarine* and *butter* are two special types of fat. Margarine is made from animal or vegetable oils or a combination of both.

Whereas other types of fats are usually bland, butter and margarine are used primarily for their characteristic flavors, which they impart to the products in which they are used. The physical properties of the fats of which they are composed are also somewhat different. This makes them "melt in the mouth," and this characteristic is imparted to the products in which they are used, particularly in icings, thus improving the quality.

*Lard,* the rendered fat of hogs, is used primarily in bread and pie dough.

*Oils* are liquid fats used, within limits, for deep fat frying in bakeries, as a wash for different types of rolls, and for greasing pans.

*Compounds* are part lard and part vegetable fat.

*Shortenings* are all those solidified fats other than lard, butter, and oleo-margarine. They do not dissolve in the liquid of the cake batter. Instead, they mix with the other ingredients, covering them uniformly with a fine film or dispersing through the mixture in fine globules. They form an emulsion with the eggs, liquids, and other ingredients.

One of the greatest advantages of using the emulsifying type of shortening in cake making is its ability to form a more stable emulsion and permit the inclusion of greater amounts of moisture and other ingredients without breaking down the batter.

To ensure that the shortenings being used will contribute high-quality characteristics to the baked product, the following points should be considered:

1. *Consistency of plasticity.* To permit shortening to function properly, it must be thoroughly and uniformly distributed in the dough or batter. It should be of a consistency that will mix easily into the dough or batter. It should also be easy to handle in the bake shop—not too hard or brittle in cold weather, or too soft in warm weather.
2. *Flavor, color, and odor* are very important. With the exception of butter, lard, and margarine, most high-grade shortenings are bland in flavor and light in color. All shortenings should be free from foreign odor.
3. *Keeping quality* of shortenings must be satisfactory under the storage conditions available in the bakery. The very best shortenings can be spoiled by rancidity when stored improperly or for too long. Shorten-

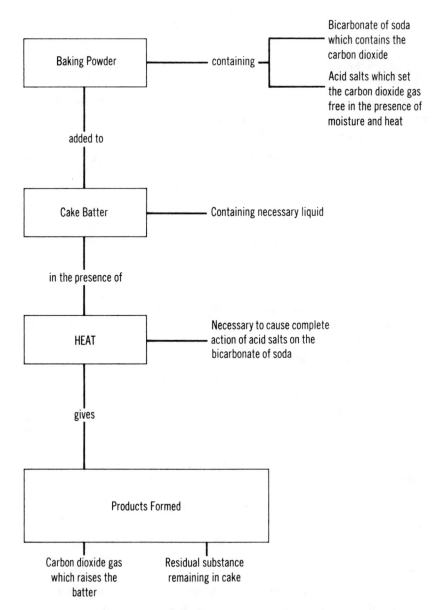

This chart is reprinted from a **Treatise on Cake Making** by permission of
Standard Brands, Inc., copyright owner.

*Figure 1.2   The action of baking powder*

ings must be kept in a cool place and tightly covered to keep out as much air as possible.

*Puff paste shortening* is used mostly in the making of Danish pastry, various puff paste articles, and as a replacement for butter in some kinds of coffee cakes. Most of the puff paste shortening is made from vegetable oils combined with hydrogenated coconut oil. The finished product then will have different degrees of hardness, depending upon the purpose for which it is intended.

### Functions of Fats in Bakery Products
Fats function in several ways in bakery products:

1. They increase the tenderness of the product.
2. They increase the quality of the product, both for keeping and eating.
3. They enhance the food value of the product.
4. They improve the grain and texture.

## FLAVORING MATERIALS

Although these materials cannot be considered as truly basic ingredients in cake making or other bakery products, they are important in producing the most desirable flavor.

Flavoring materials can be divided into three categories: extracts, emulsions, and dried spices. These and others, such as chocolate, give the desired flavor to better varieties of baked products.

*Flavoring extracts* are usually an alcoholic solution of the natural oils and other substances contained in the actual flavoring. Lemon and vanilla extracts are probably the best known and most widely used.

*Flavoring emulsions* are prepared by combining the natural oils and other substances containing the flavor with a certain amount of gum and water. Lemon flavor, as well as being used as an extract, is the most popular emulsion used in bakeries.

*Artificial flavorings* and combinations of natural and artificial flavors are produced in the form of both extracts and emulsions. Because of the potency of artificial flavors, care should be taken to avoid their excessive use.

*Spices* consist of any of the seeds, fruit, roots, buds, blossoms, or bark of certain flavor-producing plants that possess natural flavoring properties. They can lose their strength with age so they should always be kept in tightly sealed containers. The principal spices used are nutmeg, ginger, cinnamon, clove, mace, and allspice.

*Salt* may be classed as a flavoring material for our purposes. Because it intensifies other flavors, it should be mentioned as a very important flavoring material.

*Chocolate and cocoa* are derived from the cocoa bean and may be loosely classified as spices although, of course, they do not fit this classification. The principal difference in these products is the removal from cocoa of the cocoa butter, part of the natural fat, before the cocoa is powdered. Cocoa made by the Dutch process of manufacture is slightly darker and stronger in flavor than that produced by other methods.

## Use of Flavoring

Inferior flavoring material impairs the quality of any baked product and should be avoided. Excessive use, except in the case of cocoa or chocolate, is a common error. Bakers work in an atmosphere where flavoring odors are strong, and they frequently become immune to the taste and flavor. If they do not measure the quantity of flavoring material carefully, they tend to increase the amount until the product has that "bakery taste" common to some baked products.

In order to avoid the excessive use of flavoring materials, those which are particularly strong should be diluted with a suitable liquid. If the flavoring or spice is in dry form, it should be mixed with sugar. This method will permit more accurate measurement.

The flavor of the finished product is so important that it is foolish to be careless with regard to the quality and quantity of flavoring materials. Carelessness in this respect means that the baker is gambling with the loss of customers as well as with the expensive ingredients used in the product.

# CHAPTER TWO

# YEAST-MADE

# PRODUCTS

## BREAD, ROLLS, COFFEE CAKE, AND DANISH PASTRY

Bread is one of the most essential products made by bakers. It is a nutritious food, obtainable at low cost, and an essential part of every family's daily food requirement.

Many beginners in the baking trade are not enthusiastic about making bread and rolls because they feel the results are not as attractive as pastries and that breads do not produce large profits. However, the commercial bakeries are doing a fine job in giving the public excellent-quality breads.

In addition to standard breads, there are specialty breads and rolls, some of which have eye appeal and flavor to please the most fastidious gourmet. Examples of some of these may be found on the following pages.

Following are six important rules to follow in making bread and rolls.

1. Strick personal cleanliness for all employees in the bakery
2. Clean utensils, materials, and machinery
3. Use the very best quality of ingredients
4. Keep a dough thermometer on hand for controlling dough temperatures
5. Read all formulas carefully and scale all ingredients properly
6. Serve only fresh products baked daily

## BREAD AND DOUGH PRODUCTION STAGES

There are a dozen steps to baking bread, listed next. Some of them are obvious and require no further explanation; others are elaborated in the text that follows.

| | |
|---|---|
| 1. Start with raw materials | 7. Bench proofing |
| 2. Weigh ingredients | 8. Molding |
| 3. Mix | 9. Panning |
| 4. Fermentation period | 10. Pan proofing |
| 5. Scaling | 11. Baking |
| 6. Rounding | 12. Cooling |

**Dough Mixing**

There are three principal reasons for dough mixing:

1. To bring about a uniform mixture of ingredients and to form a smooth dough
2. To develop the gluten in the dough mass in order to promote the elasticity of the dough and permit it to retain the gases formed by the yeast
3. To distribute the yeast cells uniformly so that they will receive proper nutrition

There are two principal methods of mixing dough:

*Sponge dough method:* Part of the flour, water, yeast, sugar, and shortening are mixed, forming a dough called the "sponge." This is permitted to rise and ferment to the desired point. The sponge is then put back into the mixer and combined with the balance of the ingredients—the remainder of the flour, water, sugar, salt, milk, shortening, and yeast. After this is all mixed together into a smooth dough, it is again allowed to rise and divided into various-sized pieces. The sponge dough is suitable for the larger commercial operations.

*Straight dough method.* All the ingredients are placed into the mixing bowl and mixed in a single operation. The dough is then allowed to rise, the length of time depending upon the type of dough.

**Fermentation**

This takes place after the dough has been mixed and up until the time that the oven in which the dough is to be baked reaches a temperature of 138°F. At this point the yeast cells are killed and fermentation ceases.

The most favorable temperature in which fermentation can take place is 80° to 82°F. The length of the fermentation period depends upon the amount of yeast in the dough and the temperature of the room; the lower this temperature, the slower the fermentation.

A dough that is not sufficiently fermented (underproofed) is referred to as "young dough"; dough that is overproofed is known as "old dough."

The gases developed during fermentation (carbon dioxide) are forced out of the dough by a process known as "punching" the dough; this aids in relaxing the gluten and equalizes the temperature of the dough.

The best time to "punch" the dough is when it has doubled in size through fermentation. To test if the dough is ready for punching, insert the open hand into the dough four or five inches. If the dough recedes, it is ready for punching. If it springs back when the hand is inserted, longer fermentation is required. After the dough is punched, it must be proofed a second time before being made up into bread or rolls.

## Controlling Dough Temperatures

Controlling dough temperatures is very important. Proper fermentation, the quality of the finished product, and efficient production depend greatly on the temperature of the dough from the time it is mixed until it is baked.

The most desirable temperature for sponge and straight doughs range between 76° and 80°F. The exact temperature selected depends upon shop conditions and the type of bread desired. It is, therefore, highly important to calculate the required temperature of the water and the amount of ice or cooling needed to obtain the desired temperature for either sponge or straight dough.

The various types of dough mixers have different types of agitator areas and cooling devices. The machine allowance and friction differential depend on the type of mixer used as well as the amount of dough. To determine the amount of heat generated by the friction of the mixer, the following method may be used:

Mix the dough, noting the exact temperature of the flour, water, and the room. After the dough is properly mixed, note its temperature. Next, multiply the dough temperature by three, because you are working with three factors: flour, water, and room temperature. Next, subtract the sum of the three temperatures, flour, water, and room, from the dough temperature multiplied by three. The result will be the heat of the friction generated by the mixer.

|  |  |
|---|---|
| Dough temperature | 79°F |
| Multiplied by 3 | 237°F |

| Ingredients / Main Functions in Finished Product | Binding agent | Absorbing agent | Aids keeping qualities | Backbone and structure | Affects eating qualities | Nutritional value | Affects flavor | Affects fermentation | Affects gluten | Texture and grain | Imparts crust color | Affects symmetry | Volume | Produces tenderness | Adds quality to product |
|---|---|---|---|---|---|---|---|---|---|---|---|---|---|---|---|
| Bread flour | × | × | × | × | × | × | × | | | | | | | | |
| Salt | | | | | | | × | × | × | × | | | | | |
| Sugar | | | × | | × | × | × | × | | | | | | | |
| Shortening | | | × | | × | × | | | | × | × | × | | × | × |
| Milk solids | | | × | | | × | × | | | × | | | | × | × |
| Water | × | | | | | × | × | | | × | | | | | |
| Yeast | | | | | | | | | | | | | × | | |

*Figure 2.1  Bread ingredients and their functions*

| Faults \ Causes | Improper mixing | Insufficient salt | Too much salt | Dough weight too much for pan | Dough weight too light for pan | Insufficient yeast | Dough proofed too much | Dough underproofed | Dough temperature too high | Dough temperature too low | Dough too stiff | Proof box too hot | Green flour | Dough chilled | Too much sugar | Insufficient sugar | Dough too young | Dough too old | Improper molding | Insufficient shortening | Oven temperature too high | Oven temperature too low | Over-baked |
|---|---|---|---|---|---|---|---|---|---|---|---|---|---|---|---|---|---|---|---|---|---|---|---|
| Lack of volume | X | X | X | X | X | X | X |  |  |  |  |  |  | X |  |  | X | X |  | X |  |  |  |
| Too much volume |  | X | X |  |  |  |  |  |  |  |  |  |  |  |  |  |  | X |  |  | X |  |  |
| Crust color too pale |  |  |  |  |  |  |  |  |  |  | X |  |  |  |  | X |  | X |  |  |  | X |  |
| Crust color too dark |  |  |  |  |  |  |  |  | X |  |  |  |  |  | X |  | X |  |  | X | X |  |  |
| Crust blisters |  |  |  |  |  |  |  |  |  | X |  |  | X |  |  |  | X |  | X |  |  |  |  |
| Shelling of top crust |  |  |  |  |  |  |  | X |  | X |  |  |  |  |  | X | X |  |  |  |  |  |  |
| Poor keeping qualities | X |  |  |  |  |  |  | X | X |  |  |  |  |  | X |  | X | X | X |  | X |  |  |
| Poor texture, crumbly |  |  |  |  |  | X |  | X |  | X | X |  |  |  |  |  | X | X |  |  | X |  |  |
| Crust too thick |  |  |  |  |  |  |  |  |  |  |  |  |  |  |  | X |  | X |  |  | X | X |  |
| Streaky crumb |  |  |  |  |  |  |  |  |  |  |  | X |  |  |  |  |  |  | X |  |  |  |  |
| Gray crumb |  |  |  |  |  | X |  |  | X |  |  |  |  |  |  |  |  |  |  |  | X |  |  |
| Lack of shred |  |  |  |  |  | X |  |  |  |  |  |  |  |  |  |  | X | X |  |  |  |  |  |
| Coarse grain | X |  |  | X |  |  |  |  |  |  |  |  |  |  |  |  | X | X |  |  |  |  |  |
| Poor taste and flavor | X |  |  |  |  |  |  | X |  |  |  |  |  |  |  |  |  | X |  |  |  |  |  |

*Figure 2.2 Ordinary bread faults and their causes*

| | |
|---|---|
| Flour temperature | 69°F |
| Water temperature | 64°F |
| Room temperature | 79°F |
| | 212°F |
| Subtract | 237°F |
| | −212°F |
| Mixer machine friction | 25°F |

Mixing time is also an element that governs the amount of friction and should be taken into consideration when calculating temperatures. Now that the heat of the mixer friction has been established, the desired temperature of a dough with water as a chief factor must be determined.

| | |
|---|---|
| Dough temperature desired | 80°F |
| Multiplied by 3 | 240°F |
| | |
| Machine friction | 25°F |
| Flour temperature | 75°F |
| Room temperature | 75°F |
| | 175°F |
| | |
| Subtract | 240°F |
| | −175°F |
| Water temperature required | 65°F |

When a sponge dough is to be mixed, the sponge temperature must be added to the total temperature of flour, room, and mixer friction. This means working with four factors and the desired dough temperature must be multiplied by 4.

| | |
|---|---|
| Dough temperature desired | 80°F |
| Multiplied by 4 | 320°F |
| | |
| Machine friction | 25°F |
| Sponge temperature | 80°F |
| Flour temperature | 70°F |
| Room temperature | 80°F |
| | 255°F |
| | |
| Subtract | 320°F |
| | −255°F |
| Water temperature required | 65°F |

Often it is necessary to use ice to lower the water temperature to the degree required. In that case, the amount of ice necessary must be determined. For example, suppose 24 lb of water are required at a temperature of 54°F and the tap water available is 64°F. How much ice must be used?

64°F less 54°F                                  10°F
10°F multiplied by 24 lb                  240 lb

It takes 144 BTUs (British thermal units) of heat to melt 1 lb of ice to 1 lb of water. Therefore, we divide the 240 lb by 144 BTUs and find that we must use 1²/₃ lb of ice and 22¹/₃ lb of tap water at 64°F to reach a temperature of 54°F.

**Water Temperature Chart**

The chart below may be used for mixing dough with a desired dough temperature of 80°F and a machine friction of 25°F.

Read horizontally for flour temperature, vertically for room temperature. Where the two rows of figures meet determines the water temperature required. In the example below, the room temperature is 76°F and the flour temperature is 78°F. Therefore, the required water temperature is 61°F.

## ROOM TEMPERATURES

| | 90 | 88 | 86 | 84 | 82 | 80 | 78 | **76** | 74 | 72 | 70 | 68 | 66 | 64 | 62 | 60 | 58 |
|---|---|---|---|---|---|---|---|---|---|---|---|---|---|---|---|---|---|
| 90 | 35 | 37 | 39 | 41 | 43 | 45 | 47 | **49** | 51 | 53 | 55 | 57 | 59 | 61 | 63 | 65 | 67 |
| 88 | 37 | 39 | 41 | 43 | 45 | 47 | 49 | **51** | 53 | 55 | 57 | 59 | 61 | 63 | 65 | 67 | 69 |
| 86 | 39 | 41 | 43 | 45 | 47 | 49 | 51 | **53** | 55 | 57 | 59 | 61 | 63 | 65 | 67 | 69 | 71 |
| 84 | 41 | 43 | 45 | 47 | 49 | 51 | 53 | **55** | 57 | 59 | 61 | 63 | 65 | 67 | 69 | 71 | 73 |
| 82 | 43 | 45 | 47 | 49 | 51 | 53 | 55 | **57** | 59 | 61 | 63 | 65 | 67 | 69 | 71 | 73 | 75 |
| 80 | 45 | 47 | 49 | 51 | 53 | 55 | 57 | **59** | 61 | 63 | 65 | 67 | 69 | 71 | 73 | 75 | 77 |
| **78** | **47** | **49** | **51** | **53** | **55** | **57** | **59** | **(61)** | 63 | 65 | 67 | 69 | 71 | 73 | 75 | 77 | 79 |
| 76 | 49 | 51 | 53 | 55 | 57 | 59 | 61 | 63 | 65 | 67 | 69 | 71 | 73 | 75 | 77 | 79 | 81 |
| 74 | 51 | 53 | 55 | 57 | 59 | 61 | 63 | 65 | 67 | 69 | 71 | 73 | 75 | 77 | 79 | 81 | 83 |
| 72 | 53 | 55 | 57 | 59 | 61 | 63 | 65 | 67 | 69 | 71 | 73 | 75 | 77 | 79 | 81 | 83 | 85 |
| 70 | 55 | 57 | 59 | 61 | 63 | 65 | 67 | 69 | 71 | 73 | 75 | 77 | 79 | 81 | 83 | 85 | 87 |
| 68 | 57 | 59 | 61 | 63 | 65 | 67 | 69 | 71 | 73 | 75 | 77 | 79 | 81 | 83 | 85 | 87 | 89 |
| 66 | 59 | 61 | 63 | 65 | 67 | 69 | 71 | 73 | 75 | 77 | 79 | 81 | 83 | 85 | 87 | 89 | 91 |
| 64 | 61 | 63 | 65 | 67 | 69 | 71 | 73 | 75 | 77 | 79 | 81 | 83 | 85 | 87 | 89 | 91 | 93 |

(left axis label: Flour Temperatures)

DETERMINING WATER TEMPERATURES FOR MAKING BREAD

# WHITE PAN BREAD

| Bread flour | 10 lb | |
| Sugar | | 6 oz |
| Malt | | 4 oz |
| Salt | | 4 oz |
| Nonfat dry milk solids | | 8 oz |
| Water (3⅛ qt) | 6 lb | 4 oz |
| Yeast | | 8 oz |
| Shortening | | 6 oz |
| | 18 lb | 8 oz |

*Method:* Straight dough. 1 hour fermentation period.
*Baking instructions:* 400°F.

# RYE BREAD

| Rye blend flour | 5 lb | |
| Salt | | 2 oz |
| Sugar | | 2 oz |
| Shortening | | 2 oz |
| Water (1½ qt) | 3 lb | |
| Yeast | | 4 oz |
| Caraway seeds | | 1 oz |
| Rye flavor* | | 1 oz |
| | 8 lb | 12 oz |

*Method:* Straight dough. Mix for 5 minutes at second speed. Desired dough temperature, 80°F. 1 hour fermentation period.
*Scaling instructions:* Rolls: 1 lb per dozen. Bread: 1 lb per loaf.
*Baking instructions:* 400°F with steam for the first 10 minutes.

*May be omitted

# J E W I S H   C H A L A H

| | | |
|---|---|---|
| Bread flour | 5 lb | |
| Salt | | 1 1/2 oz |
| Sugar or malt | | 4 oz |
| Oil | | 4 oz |
| Egg yolks, 6 | | 4 oz |
| Yeast | | 3 oz |
| Water (1 3/8 qt) | 2 lb | 12 oz |
| | 8 lb | 12 1/2 oz |

*Method:* Straight dough. Mix for approximately 12 minutes at second speed. Desired dough temperature, 80°F. 1 hour fermentation period. Egg wash before baking. Braiding instructions follow on Figures 2.3 through 2.7.

*Scaling instructions:* 1 lb per loaf.

*Baking instructions:* 400°F.

# W H O L E   W H E A T   B R E A D   A N D   R O L L S

| | | |
|---|---|---|
| Whole wheat flour | 5 lb | |
| Salt | | 2 oz |
| Sugar | | 8 oz |
| Shortening | | 8 oz |
| Milk solids | | 4 oz |
| Water (1 11/16 qt) | 3 lb | 6 oz |
| Yeast | | 4 oz |
| | 10 lb | |

*Method:* Straight dough. Mix approximately 12 minutes at medium speed. Desired dough temperature, 80° F. 1 hour fermentation period. Remove from pans after baking.

*Scaling instructions:* Rolls: 1 lb per dozen. Bread: 1 lb per loaf.

*Baking instructions:* 400°F.

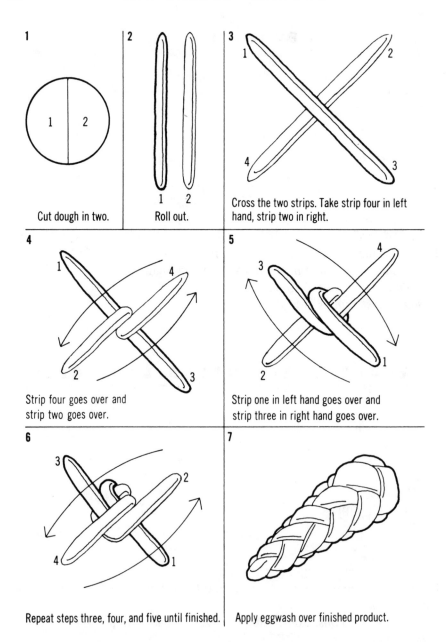

**1**

1 | 2

Cut dough in two.

**2**

1   2

Roll out.

**3**

1          2

4          3

Cross the two strips. Take strip four in left hand, strip two in right.

**4**

1          4

2          3

Strip four goes over and strip two goes over.

**5**

3          4

2          1

Strip one in left hand goes over and strip three in right hand goes over.

**6**

3          2

4          1

Repeat steps three, four, and five until finished.

**7**

Apply eggwash over finished product.

*Figure 2.3   Steps for making two-braided bread*

**1** Cut dough as illustrated.

**2** Roll out in strips.
1 2 3  4 5 6

**3**
1  2  3

**4** Three over two
1  3  2

**5** One over three
3  1  2

**6** Two over one
3  2  1

**7** Three over two
2  3  1

**8** One over three
2  1  3

**9** One end finished

**10** Flip over.

**11** Repeat steps four through ten with smaller strips
A
B

**12** Egg wash (A) and place bread strips (B) on top.

*Figure 2.4   Steps for making three-braided bread*

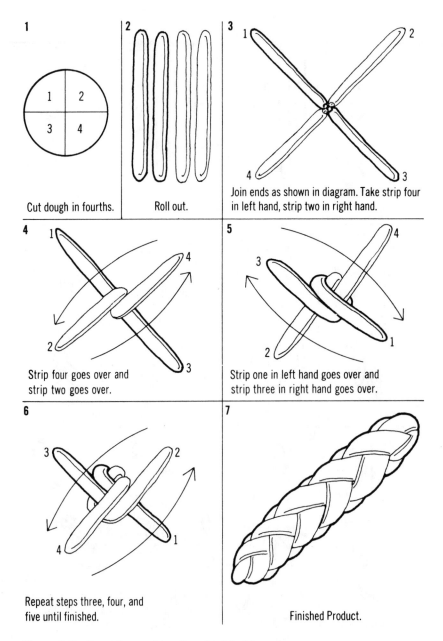

**1**

1 | 2
3 | 4

Cut dough in fourths.

**2**

Roll out.

**3**

Join ends as shown in diagram. Take strip four in left hand, strip two in right hand.

**4**

Strip four goes over and strip two goes over.

**5**

Strip one in left hand goes over and strip three in right hand goes over.

**6**

Repeat steps three, four, and five until finished.

**7**

Finished Product.

*Figure 2.5   Steps for making four-braided bread*

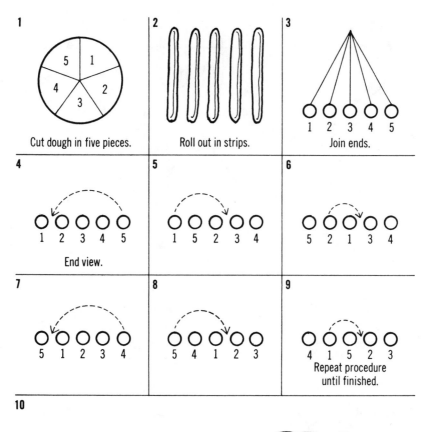

**1** Cut dough in five pieces.

**2** Roll out in strips.

**3** Join ends. 1 2 3 4 5

**4** End view. 1 2 3 4 5

**5** 1 5 2 3 4

**6** 5 2 1 3 4

**7** 5 1 2 3 4

**8** 5 4 1 2 3

**9** 4 1 5 2 3 Repeat procedure until finished.

**10**

Finished Product.

*Figure 2.6 Steps for making five-braided bread*

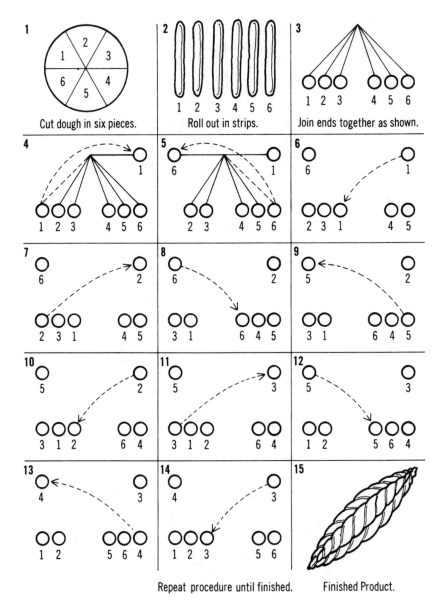

Figure 2.7   *Steps for making six-braided bread*

## PUMPERNICKEL BREAD

| | | |
|---|---|---|
| Rye flour | 2 lb | 8 oz |
| Bread flour, clear | 2 lb | 8 oz |
| Rye meal | 1 lb | 8 oz |
| Salt | | 2 oz |
| Sugar or malt | | 2 oz |
| Water (2 qt) | 4 lb | |
| Yeast | | 3 oz |
| Rye flour | | 1 oz |
| | 11 lb | |

*Method:* Straight dough. Mix approximately 5 minutes at medium speed. Desired dough temperature, 80°F. 30 minute fermentation period. Wash with paste of rye and water before baking. Punch holes before baking.

*Baking instructions:* 400°F with steam the first 10 minutes.

## HOLLAND DUTCH TOPPING

| | | |
|---|---|---|
| Rice flour | | 14 oz |
| Sugar | | 1 oz |
| Shortening | | 1 1/2 oz |
| Salt | | 1/2 oz |
| Yeast | | 1 1/2 oz |
| Warm water (1 1/2 pints) | 1 lb | 8 oz |
| | 2 lb | 10 1/2 oz |

*Method:* Dissolve yeast in warm water. Add to dry ingredients. Let rise one time and apply to rolls or bread.

### Cornucopia

The cornucopia or horn of plenty is made from bread dough, using the hard roll dough recipe, but without the yeast. This method for making the cornucopia is rather new and unique; the dough is not rolled out manually, but is extruded through a meat grinder, with a sausage funnel attached to it in order for the dough to be symmetrically shaped. The form for the cornucopia can be made in any size, using chicken wire covered with aluminum foil. The dough is wrapped around the form of the cornucopia. Note that the dough is started from the small end, working toward the large opening of the cornucopia. It is recommended that a rich egg wash be used over the dough before baking. A good glaze for the finished cornucopia can be prepared by using 1/2 ounce of granulated powdered gelatin and 1 pint of water. The gelatin should be heated and dissolved and brushed or applied directly on the cornucopia directly after it comes out of the oven. This will give the product a shiny effect.

## HARD ROLL DOUGH

| | | |
|---|---|---|
| Bread flour | 5 lb | |
| Salt | | 2 oz |
| Sugar | | 2 oz |
| Shortening | | 2 oz |
| Egg whites | | 2 oz |
| Water (1 1/2 qt) | 3 lb | |
| Yeast | | 3 oz |
| | 8 lb | 11 oz |

*Method:* Straight dough. Mix approximately 12 minutes at second speed. Desired dough temperature, 80°F. 1 hour fermentation period.

*Scaling instructions:* Hard rolls: 1 lb per dozen. Bread: 1 lb per loaf.

*Baking instructions:* 400°F with steam for approximately the first 10 minutes.

*Variations:* This dough may be used for a variety of hard rolls, French bread, Vienna bread, or Italian bread.

## HOMEMADE EGG NOODLES

| | | |
|---|---|---|
| Bread flour | 5 lb | |
| Eggs, 16 | 1 lb | 8 oz |
| Salt | | 2 oz |
| Oil | | 1 oz |
| Water (1 pint) | 1 lb | |
| | 7 lb | 11 oz |

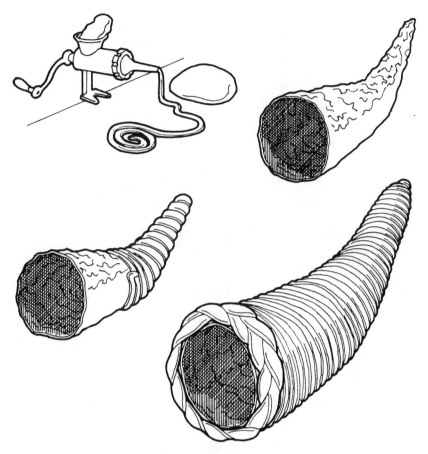

*Figure 2.8   Steps in making a cornucopia*

*Method:* Mix into a smooth dough and let relax for approximately one-half hour before rolling. Let dry and cut. This dough lends itself to the making of baskets and horns of plenty.

## WEAVING BREAD OR NOODLE BASKETS

The art of weaving bread or noodle dough requires patient practice. Many important points influence the finished product.

Most important is to have a well-made frame or board. There should be an uneven number of holes, as shown in Figure 2.9. There are always an uneven number of pegs spread approximately three-quarters of an inch to one-inch apart, and these are set at a slight angle so that the basket is larger

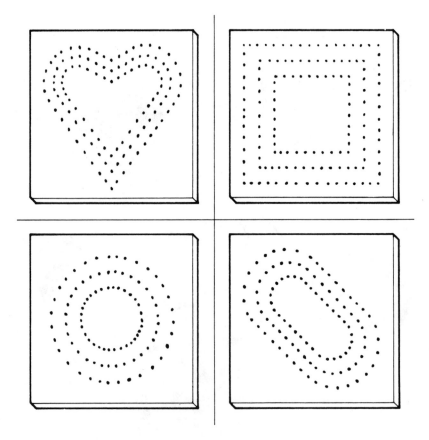

*Figure 2.9   Boards for weaving bread baskets; each row is for a different size of basket.*

at the top than at the bottom. Note that there are three different graduated-size holes in the illustrations.

The dough being used must be rolled evenly and woven around the wooden pegs for uniformity.

Before baking, brush with a straight egg wash. The handle may be made with wire. Weave the dough around the wire, bake, and then set onto the basket.

*Figure 2.10   Weaving a bread basket*

## SOFT ROLL DOUGH

| Bread flour | 5 lb | |
|---|---|---|
| Salt | | 2 oz |
| Sugar | | 8 oz |
| Shortening | | 8 oz |
| Milk solids | | 4 oz |
| Water (1½ qt) | 3 lb | |
| Yeast | | 4 oz |
| | 9 lb | 10 oz |

*Method:* Straight dough. Mix approximately 12 minutes at medium speed. Desired dough temperature, 80°F. 1 hour fermentation period.

*Scaling instructions:* 12 oz per dozen rolls. Yield: 12½ dozen.

*Baking instructions:* 400°F.

## DANISH PASTRY DOUGH

| Salt | | 1 oz |
|---|---|---|
| Sugar | 1 lb | |
| Butter | 2 lb | 10 oz |
| Eggs | 1 lb | |
| Milk (1 qt) | 2 lb | |
| Yeast | | 4 oz |
| Bread flour | 4 lb | 8 oz |
| Cake flour | | 8 oz |
| | 11 lb | 15 oz |

*Method:* Mix all ingredients but 2 lb of butter into a straight dough. Roll the 2 lb of butter into the dough. After mixing, retard 10 to 15 minutes. Then sheet out dough to a thickness of 1/2 to 3/4 inch, three times as long as wide. Spot butter over 2/3 the length of the dough sheet. Fold the third without butter over the center third. Fold the remaining third on top, making three layers of dough, two layers with butter. Again allow the dough to rest 20 to 30 minutes in the retarder. This rolling and folding must be repeated twice more. After rolling out for the last time, it is advisable to allow the dough to rest in the retarder for 4 or 5 hours before making up into varieties. Proofing before baking should be with little steam and at 90° to 95°F.

*Baking instructions:* 375°F.

## B A N A N A   B R E A D

| Sugar | 2 lb | |
|---|---|---|
| Shortening | 1 lb | |
| Salt | | 1 oz |
| Eggs, beaten | 1 lb | 8 oz |
| Bananas, mashed | 2 lb | 8 oz |
| Cake flour | 3 lb | |
| Cream of tartar | | 1 oz |
| Baking soda | | 1 oz |
| | 10 lb | 3 oz |

*Method:* Cream together sugar, shortening, and salt. Add beaten eggs and bananas. Sift together flour, cream of tartar, and baking soda; add to other ingredients and mix together until smooth.

*Scaling instructions:* 1 1/2 lb per loaf.

*Baking instructions:* 375°F.

1. Dough.

2. Cut off two slices.

3. Form as shown.

4. Assemble as shown.

5. Cut as shown. Use raisins for eyes. Slit mouth with shears and prop open with foil.

6. Finished bread Alligator.

*Figure 2.11   Bread alligator*

# SWEET DOUGH

| Ingredient | | |
|---|---|---|
| Salt | | 1 oz |
| Sugar | 1 lb | |
| Shortening and butter | 1 lb | |
| Flavor and spice (to taste) | | |
| Eggs | | 12 oz |
| Milk (1 qt) | 2 lb | |
| Yeast | | 6 oz |
| Bread flour | 3 lb | 8 oz |
| Cake flour | 1 lb | |
| | 9 lb | 11 oz |

*Method:* Mix into a straight dough. 1 1/2 hour fermentation period. Desired dough temperature, 80°F.

*Baking instructions:* 375°F.

# DATE AND NUT BREAD

| Ingredient | | |
|---|---|---|
| Brown sugar | 1 lb | |
| Shortening | | 8 oz |
| Salt | | 1 oz |
| Eggs | | 12 oz |
| Baking soda | | 1 oz |
| Water (1 qt) | 2 lb | |
| Bread flour | 2 lb | |
| Whole wheat flour | 1 lb | |
| Baking powder | | 1 oz |
| Dates, soaked and chopped | 2 lb | |
| Walnuts | 1 lb | |
| | 10 lb | 7 oz |

*Method:* Cream together sugar, shortening, and salt. Beat in eggs. Dissolve baking soda in water and add. Sift together flours and baking powder, add to mixture, and mix until smooth. Flour dates, and then stir into dough with walnuts.

*Scaling instructions:* 1 lb 6 oz per loaf.

*Baking instructions:* 375°F.

Dough.

Cut off three slices.

Form the above five pieces.

Assemble as shown using raisins for eyes.

Score back.

Finished bread turtle.

*Figure 2.12   Bread turtle*

## C O R N   B R E A D

| | | |
|---|---|---|
| Cornmeal | 2 lb | 4 oz |
| Pastry flour | 1 lb | 8 oz |
| Sugar | | 4 oz |
| Baking powder | | 1 ½ oz |
| Salt | | 1 ½ oz |
| Milk (1 ½ qt) | 3 lb | |
| Eggs | | 12 oz |
| Butter, melted | | 12 oz |
| | 8 lb | 11 oz |

*Method:* Sift cornmeal, flour, sugar, baking powder, and salt, and blend together. Beat milk and eggs together and add. Add melted butter and mix smooth. Pour mixture into greased sheet pans.

*Scaling instructions:* 9 lb 7 oz for one 18 × 24-inch sheet pan.

*Baking instructions:* 450°F. Serve hot.

## C O R N   B R E A D
## A N D   C O R N   B R E A D   S T I C K S

| | | |
|---|---|---|
| Salt | | 2 oz |
| Sugar | | 3 oz |
| Shortening | | 8 oz |
| Cake flour | 2 lb | 8 oz |
| Yellow cornmeal | 2 lb | 8 oz |
| Baking powder | | 5 oz |
| Eggs, whole | 1 lb | 8 oz |
| Buttermilk (2 qt) | 4 lb | |
| | 11 lb | 10 oz |

*Method:* Blend salt, sugar, shortening, flour, cornmeal, and baking powder and mix. Beat in eggs and 2 lb of buttermilk until mixture is smooth. Add rest of buttermilk and mix with above in three parts. Press into corn sticks with star tube.

## BASIC FRUIT MUFFINS

| | | |
|---|---|---|
| Sugar, powdered | 1 lb | |
| Shortening and butter | | 8 oz |
| Salt | | 1/2 oz |
| Eggs | 1 lb | |
| Milk (1 pint) | 1 lb | |
| Baking powder | | 1 oz |
| Cake flour | 1 lb | 12 oz |
| Fruit or nuts | 1 lb | 8 oz |
| | 6 lb | 13 1/2 oz |

*Method:* Cream together sugar, shortening, and salt. Add eggs, then milk. Sift baking powder and flour together and mix into mixture until smooth. Fold fruit or nuts into mixture.

*Scaling instructions:* 18 oz per dozen.

*Baking instructions:* 400°F.


## BAKING POWDER BISCUITS

| | | |
|---|---|---|
| Cake flour | 2 lb | |
| Salt | | 1 oz |
| Baking powder | | 2 oz |
| Shortening and butter | | 12 oz |
| Milk (1 1/4 pints) | 1 lb | 4 oz |
| | 4 lb | 3 oz |

*Method:* Sift and blend flour, salt, and baking powder. Rub in shortening and butter. Add milk and mix smooth.

*Scaling instructions:* Approximately 4 dozen 2-inch biscuits.

*Baking instructions:* 400°F.

1 = Long pumpernickel. 2 = Italian bread. 3 = American rye. 4 = Pullman loaf. 5 = Round cinnamon loaf. 6 = Braided loaf. 7 = French loaf. 8 = Jewish Challah. 9 = Six-strand braided loaf.
10 = Vienna loaf. 11 = Round pumpernickel. 12 = White Mountain bread. 13 = White pan bread.

*Figure 2.13   Varieties of bread*

## BRIOCHES

| | | |
|---|---|---|
| Flour | 1 lb | 8 oz |
| Yeast | | 2 oz |
| Milk (1 pint) | 1 lb | |
| Salt | | 1 oz |
| Sugar | | 2 oz |
| Butter | 1 lb | 4 oz |
| Eggs | | 12 oz |
| Flour | 1 lb | 12 oz |
| | 6 lb | 9 oz |

*Method:* Make a sponge of flour, yeast, and milk and let rise. Mix in remaining ingredients until smooth. Place in the refrigerator overnight.

*Scaling instructions:* 1½ oz per unit.

*Baking instructions:* 375°F.

## POPOVERS

| | | |
|---|---|---|
| Eggs | | 8 oz |
| Milk (1 pint) | 1 lb | |
| Salt | | ½ oz |
| Sugar | | ½ oz |
| Bread flour | | 12 oz |
| | 2 lb | 5 oz |

*Method:* Beat well together eggs, milk, salt, and sugar. Add flour and mix until smooth.

*Scaling instructions:* Grease every other cup of muffin pan to allow for expansion of popovers. Fill muffin cups ¾ full. Only 6 popovers should be placed in the pan instead of the full 12. Yield: 36 medium-size popovers.

*Baking instructions:* 400°–425°F for 10 minutes. Reduce heat to 375°F for additional 20 minutes. Be sure to dry popovers sufficiently before removing from oven to prevent them from collapsing.

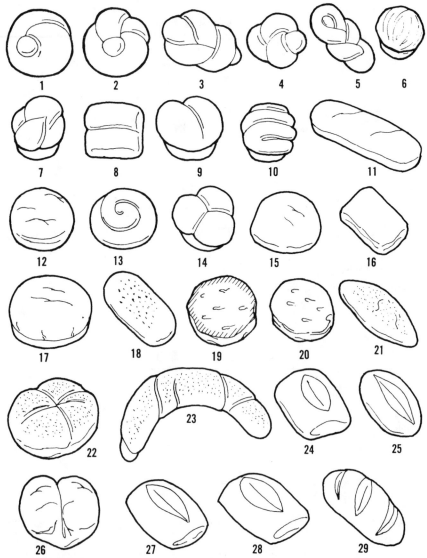

**Soft rolls:** 1 = Single knot. 2 = Double knot. 3 = Figure eight. 4 = Square knot. 5 = Braided roll. 6 = Spiral butter roll. 7 = Butter twist. 8 = Parker house roll. 9 = Twin roll. 10 = Butter roll. 11 = Frankfurter roll. 12 = Whole wheat roll. 13 = Spiral roll. 14 = Clover leaf roll. 15 = Pan roll. 16 = Snowflake roll. 17 = Hamburger roll. 18 = Poppyseed roll. 19 = Maryland roll with flour top. 20 = Vienna roll without flour top. 21 = Vienna bridge roll. **Hard rolls:** 22 = Kaiser roll. 23 = Crescent roll. 24 = French roll. 25 = Rye roll. 26 = Water roll. 27 = Small French roll. 28 = Club roll. 29 = Rye roll.

*Figure 2.14   Varieties of rolls*

## W A F F L E S

| | | |
|---|---|---|
| Eggs | | 6 oz |
| Sugar (variable) | | 2 oz |
| Salt | | 1/4 oz |
| Milk (1 pint) | 1 lb | |
| Cake flour | 1 lb | |
| Baking powder | | 1 oz |
| Butter, melted | | 4 oz |
| | 2 lb | 13 1/4 oz |

*Method:* Beat together eggs, sugar, and salt. Add milk. Sift flour and baking powder, and stir in until batter is smooth. Add melted butter.

*Variation:* For cornmeal waffles, replace 4 oz of flour with 4 oz of cornmeal.

## G I N G E R B R E A D   W A F F L E S

| | | |
|---|---|---|
| Molasses | 1 lb | |
| Shortening | | 5 oz |
| Eggs, 4 | | |
| Salt | | 1/4 oz |
| Baking soda | | 1/2 oz |
| Ginger | | 3/4 oz |
| Buttermilk (1/2 pint) | | 8 oz |
| Pastry flour | 1 lb | |
| | 2 lb | 14 1/2 oz |

*Method:* Melt shortening and mix with molasses. Whip together eggs, salt, baking soda, and ginger, and add to molasses mixture. Add buttermilk. Sift flour, add to mixture, and mix smooth. Waffle iron should be slightly cooler for this type of waffle.

## GRIDDLE CAKES

| | | |
|---|---|---|
| Eggs, 3 | | 5 oz |
| Salt | | 1/4 oz |
| Sugar (variable) | | 1 oz |
| Milk (1 1/2 pints) | 1 lb | 8 oz |
| Cake flour | 1 lb | |
| Baking powder | | 1 oz |
| Butter, melted | | 2 oz |
| | 3 lb | 1 1/4 oz |

*Method:* Beat together the eggs, salt, and sugar. Add milk. Sift flour and baking powder and blend with other ingredients. Add melted butter and mix in well. Care should be taken not to overmix griddle cake batter as this tends to make them tough.

## FRENCH CRESCENTS

| | | |
|---|---|---|
| Milk (1 qt) | 2 lb | |
| Yeast | | 3 oz |
| Salt | | 1 1/4 oz |
| Sugar | | 3 oz |
| Butter | | 5 oz |
| Bread flour | 3 lb | 8 oz |
| Butter | 1 lb | 8 oz |
| | 7 lb | 12 1/4 oz |

*Method:* Mix all ingredients except the butter and stir into a smooth dough. Roll butter into the dough, giving three turns as for Danish. Allow to rest in refrigerator overnight. Roll pieces into crescent shapes, proof in proofing cabinet, and bake.

*Scaling instructions:* 1 1/2 oz per unit.

*Baking instructions:* 375°F.

## BOSTON BROWN BREAD

| | | |
|---|---|---|
| Bread flour | 1 lb | |
| Rye flour | 1 lb | |
| Whole wheat flour | 1 lb | |
| Cornmeal | 1 lb | |
| Salt | | 2 oz |
| Cream of tartar | | 1 oz |
| Molasses | 1 lb | |
| Eggs | | 4 oz |
| Milk (2 qt) | 4 lb | |
| Baking soda | | 2 oz |
| | 9 lb | 9 oz |

*Method:* Sift and blend the flours and cornmeal, salt, and cream of tartar. Beat together molasses, eggs, and 3 lb of milk, and add to dry ingredients. Dissolve the baking soda in the rest of the milk and mix smooth.

*Scaling instructions:* Line pans with paper, 4 lb 8 oz per $4\frac{1}{2} \times 4\frac{1}{2} \times 14\frac{1}{2}$-inch pan. Fill pans approximately two-thirds full.

*Baking instructions:* Steam 2 hours at 450°F.

*Raisin brown bread:* Add 1 lb of raisins.

## CORN MUFFINS AND CORN STICKS

| | | |
|---|---|---|
| Sugar | 1 lb | |
| Shortening | | 8 oz |
| Salt | | $\frac{1}{2}$ oz |
| Eggs | | 8 oz |
| Milk (1 $\frac{1}{2}$ pints) | 1 lb | 8 oz |
| Cornmeal | 1 lb | |
| Pastry flour | 1 lb | 8 oz |
| Baking powder | | 1 $\frac{1}{2}$ oz |
| | 6 lb | 2 oz |

*Method:* Cream sugar, shortening, and salt. Beat in eggs and stir in milk. Add cornmeal. Sift flour and baking powder mix into above until smooth.

*Scaling instructions:* 1$\frac{1}{2}$ lb per dozen. Yield: Approximately 4 dozen muffins or 6 dozen corn sticks.

*Baking instructions:* 425°F.

## PIZZA DOUGH

| Bread flour | 3 lb | |
|---|---|---|
| Salt | | 1 oz |
| Oil or shortening | | 4 oz |
| Yeast* | | 1 1/2 oz |
| Water (1 qt) | 2 lb | |
| | 5 lb | 6 1/2 oz |

*Method:* Combine ingredients. Mix together for 10 minutes until dough becomes stretchy. After mixing dough place in an oiled pot or bowl and allow dough to rise for approximately one hour.

*Yield:* Seven 12-oz pizzas.

## PIZZA SAUCE

| Italian plum tomatoes | 2 No. 3 cans |
|---|---|
| Tomato puree | 1/2 No. 3 can |
| Garlic, chopped fine | 1/4 clove |
| Salt (to taste) | |
| Tabasco | 3/4 teaspoon |
| Oregano | 3/4 teaspoon |

*Method:* Put the Italian plum tomatoes through a food grinder with a medium cutter. Combine all ingredients and stir together.

*Yield:* Sauce for 12 pizzas.

*Directions for making pizza*

1. After dough has fermented, scale dough into 12-oz pieces or any desired weight.
2. Knead and shape dough pieces into round balls and set aside to proof for at least 30 minutes. (Cover with a dry cloth during this period.)
3. Spread these dough pieces by hand into mounds of 14- to 16-inch diameter. Stretch from the center to outer edges.

*Yeast may vary according to length of fermentation desired.

4. Over these rounds of dough that have been prepared, spread tomato sauce, and sprinkle with grated cheese. Then spread some olive oil over entire top of pizza.
5. Place in a very hot oven 500°–550°F and bake for 10 to 12 minutes.

*Variations:* Anchovies, onions, mozzarella cheese, chicken, sliced sausage, mushrooms, and bacon are popular. These toppings go over the sauce and not directly on the dough.

## BRAN MUFFINS

| | | |
|---|---|---|
| Sugar | 1 lb | |
| Shortening | | 8 oz |
| Salt | | 1/2 oz |
| Eggs | 1 lb | |
| Milk (1 1/2 pints) | 1 lb | 8 oz |
| Bran | | 8 oz |
| Bread flour | 1 lb | 8 oz |
| Baking powder | | 1 1/2 oz |
| Honey and molasses | | 8 oz |
| | 6 lb | 10 oz |

*Method:* Cream together sugar, shortening, and salt. Stir in, one after the other, eggs, milk, and bran. Sift together flour and baking powder and mix into batter until smooth. Add honey and molasses to the mixture.
*Scaling instructions:* 1 1/2 lb per dozen. Yield: Approximately 4 dozen.
*Baking instructions:* 425°F.

*Variation:* 1 lb of raisins may be added to this mixture to make raisin bran muffins.

## HONEY GLAZE FOR DOUGHNUTS

| | | |
|---|---|---|
| Confectioners' sugar | 10 lb | |
| Honey | | 8 oz |
| Salt | | 1/2 oz |
| Vanilla (to taste) | | |
| Water (1 1/8 qt) | 2 lb | 4 oz |
| Gelatin | | 3/4 oz |
| | 12 lb | 13 1/4 oz |

*Method:* Heat water and gelatin to 160°F and mix with other ingredients until smooth. Dip doughnuts into glaze while they are hot.

## COFFEE CAKE TOPPINGS AND FILLINGS

## CINNAMON SUGAR

| | | |
|---|---|---|
| Sugar | 1 lb | |
| Cinnamon (variable) | | 1/2 oz |
| | 1 lb | 1/2 oz |

*Method:* Blend together. Sprinkle over top of cake.

## DATE FILLING

| | | |
|---|---|---|
| Dates, ground | 2 lb | |
| Brown sugar | | 8 oz |
| Water (1 pint) | 1 lb | |
| | 3 lb | 8 oz |

*Method:* Soak dates in water used in filling for 1 hour before grinding. Boil and stir for 10 minutes. Cool before using.

*Date and nut:* Add 8 oz of chopped nuts to the above mixture.

# MELTAWAY FILLING

| | | |
|---|---|---|
| Confectioners' sugar | 2 lb | |
| Butter and shortening | 1 lb | |
| Milk solids | | 1 oz |
| Egg whites | | 2 oz |
| | 3 lb | 3 oz |

*Method:* Cream together sugar, shortening, and milk solids. Add egg whites and cream lightly.

# STREUSEL TOPPING

| | |
|---|---|
| Butter and shortening | 1 lb |
| Sugar | 1 lb |
| Cake and bread flour | 2 lb |
| Mace or cinnamon flavor (to taste) | |
| | 4 lb |

*Method:* Rub together until as crumbly as desired.

*Variation:* Add 4 oz of chopped almonds.

# ALMOND FILLING

| | | |
|---|---|---|
| Almond paste | 1 lb | |
| Sugar | 1 lb | |
| Butter and shortening | | 8 oz |
| Pastry flour | | 4 oz |
| Eggs | | 4 oz |
| | 3 lb | |

*Method:* Mix almond paste and sugar. Blend flour and shortening and add to first mixture, beating until smooth. Add eggs and blend until smooth.

*Cherry almond filling:* Add 8 oz chopped glacé cherries to above.
*Chocolate almond filling:* Add 4 oz chocolate instead of pastry flour.

## CHEESE FILLING

| | | |
|---|---|---|
| Baker's cheese | 1 lb | |
| Sugar | | 4 oz |
| Salt | | 1/4 oz |
| Eggs, 2 | | 3 oz |
| Butter, melted | | 2 oz |
| | 1 lb | 9 1/4 oz |

*Method:* Mix all together. Spread over pastry.

*Pineapple Cheese:* Add 4 oz crushed pineapple.

## PEANUT BUTTER FILLING

| | | |
|---|---|---|
| Brown sugar | 12 oz | |
| Peanut butter | 12 oz | |
| Salt | 1/2 oz | |
| Butter | 12 oz | |
| Cake crumbs, toasted | 12 oz | |
| Eggs | 4 oz | |
| Water | 12 oz | |
| | 4 lb | 1/2 oz |

*Method:* Mix all ingredients together thoroughly.

## POPPY SEED FILLING

| | | |
|---|---|---|
| Poppy seeds | 1 lb | |
| Water | | 8 oz |
| Honey | | 2 oz |
| Sugar | | 8 oz |
| Butter | | 4 oz |
| Lemon rind (from 1 lemon) | | 1/4 oz |
| Cake crumbs | 1 lb | |
| Salt | | 1/4 oz |
| Eggs | | 3 oz |
| | 3 lb | 9 1/2 oz |

*Method:* Soak poppy seeds in water for 8 hours and grind fine. Add remaining ingredients.

## HONEY PAN GLAZE

| | | |
|---|---|---|
| Brown sugar | 2 lb | |
| Butter and shortening | 1 lb | |
| Malt | | 8 oz |
| Honey | | 8 oz |
| Water | | 4 oz |
| | 4 lb | 4 oz |

*Method:* Cream together all ingredients.

## SHINY GLAZE FOR COFFEE CAKE AND DANISH

| | |
|---|---|
| Corn syrup | 3 lb |
| Water (1 pint) | 1 lb |
| | 4 lb |

*Method:* Boil together and apply while hot.

# ICING FOR COFFEE CAKE AND DANISH

| | | |
|---|---|---|
| Confectioners' sugar | 5 lb | |
| Corn syrup | | 4 oz |
| Hot water (variable) | | 10 oz |
| Egg whites | | 1 oz |
| Vanilla or lemon flavoring (to taste) | | |
| | 5 lb | 15 oz |

*Method:* Mix all ingredients together thoroughly.

# CHAPTER THREE

# CAKES AND TORTES

If uniform results are to be obtained in caking making, the careful weighing of ingredients is absolutely essential. Every bakeshop must have a good scale that will weigh from fractions of ounces up to several pounds. This is particularly necessary for leavening agents and flavorings. Accurate scaling prevents fluctuations in the quality of the products from day to day.

## MIXING CAKE BATTERS

Extreme care must be taken in the handling and mixing of cake batter. Each type of cake batter should be mixed in accordance with a specific formula. Every phase of the mixing method must be carefully observed.

The three principal ways to mix cake batters are the creaming method, the two-stage method, and the sponge or foam method.

### Creaming Method

1. Weigh all ingredients carefully and keep all of them at room temperature.
2. Sugar, shortening or butter, salt, flavors, and spices are usually creamed together.
3. Add required amount of eggs gradually in small amounts, and continue to cream.
4. Add liquids (milk or water as directed) very gradually. In some batters,

it is advisable to add only a portion of the liquid alternately with the flour.

5. Add sifted baking powder and flour, and mix until a smooth batter is obtained.

6. Throughout the entire mixing process, the sides of the bowl should be scraped down occasionally to ensure a uniform batter.

**Two-Stage Method**

1. Weigh all ingredients carefully and keep all of them at room temperature.

2. Place all dry ingredients in a mixing bowl—flour, sugar, spices, baking powder, salt, and any other dry ingredients. Add the shortening and part of the milk and mix at a slow speed for the required amount of time.

3. Add the required amount of eggs to the balance of the milk. Beat slightly and add this to the above mixture in about three parts, scraping the sides of the bowl at intervals.

**Sponge or Foam Method**

1. Scale all ingredients carefully. All should be at room temperature.

2. Warm eggs and sugar to about 100°F. This dissolves the sugar. Beat until the required temperature is reached.

3. Fold in flour to ensure uniformity.

There are variations to these basic methods. Every formula for cake making should include complete mixing methods.

## HIGH-ALTITUDE CAKE BAKING

Almost all formulas released for general distribution to the baking industry are developed in cities at low altitude. The various ingredients in the formulas are balanced with each other so that they produce the desired results at or near sea level. It is recognized, however, that at high altitudes (because of lessened atmospheric pressure) the same formulas must be adjusted to perform satisfactorily.

Those who have baked at higher altitudes have usually followed adjustments worked out through experience on the basis of the older, lower-sugar formulas. Generally, these changes for batter cakes consist of reducing the baking powder and sugar and increasing the liquid as the altitude increases. Such an adjustment protected the physical character of the cakes, but necessarily lowered their eating quality and flavor. As mentioned before, cakes are sweet desserts, and anything that markedly lowers their sweetness detracts from their general appeal and acceptability.

General Mills has carried out extensive work on cake baking at higher altitudes. The results of these tests indicate that with the emulsifier type of shortening and softer cake batters, it is not necessary at higher altitudes to reduce the sugar percentage from sea-level amounts if the sugar percentage ranges from approximately 120 to 130%, based on flour. This is particularly true in cakes made by the two-stage method, where by standardized shop manipulation, it is possible to control to a large degree the amount of air incorporated in the batter.

It is to be expected that some experimental baking will have to be done to adapt a sea-level formula to the particular elevation of any individual shop and to meet the local conditions that may prevail. Figure 3.1 is offered as a guide toward minimizing this unavoidable experimentation.

Because of the lowering of atmospheric pressure as altitude increases and the tremendous effect it has on cake baking, we find that the three ingredients that require adjustment to compensate for this condition are leavening materials, eggs, and flour.

*Leavening materials.* Reduce baking powder, soda, cream of tartar, or other agents having leavening action in the cakes, beginning at 2000 feet elevation (making a 15% reduction at this elevation), and increase the reduction as the altitude increases, until at 8000 feet elevation the reduction amounts to 60% of the quantity used at sea level. For example, if a cake formula developed at sea level calls for 5 oz of baking powder, at 8000 feet elevation only 2 oz should be used.

If a dark cake formula at sea level calls for soda, buttermilk, and/or baking powder, the correction of the leavening agents can best be controlled and adjusted by changing to sweet milk and baking powder only. This eliminates the compensations involved in considering more than one gas-producing leavening ingredient.

It is also suggested that the creaming of the shortening and sugar be standardized both as to machine speed and time so that the volume of air incorporated into the batter will be as uniform as possible. In this manner the volume of the cakes can be controlled and their rapid drying or crumbling can be materially lessened.

*Eggs.* Beginning at 2500 feet elevation, add 2½% more whole eggs or egg whites. Gradually increase the egg content as the elevation increases, until at 7500 feet 15% more is used. For example, if a formula developed at sea

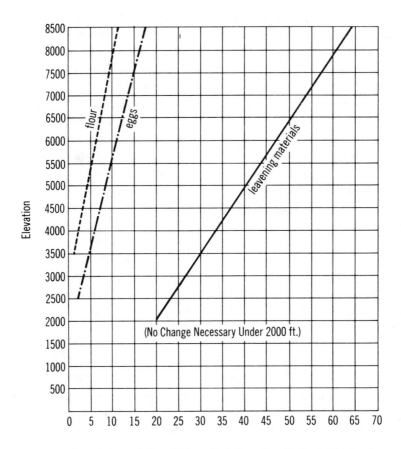

Percent change in Essential Ingredients From Amounts Used at Sea Level

*Figure 3.1   Relationship of altitude to the amount of essential ingredients used in cakes.*

level specified 2 lb 8 oz (40 oz) whole eggs, at 2500 feet elevation use 1 oz more, or 2 lb 9 oz. At 7500 feet elevation use a total of 2 lb 14 oz. By increasing the eggs, more liquid is added to the mix and at the same time greater stability is provided, due to the strengthening action of the egg protein.

*Flour.* Beginning at 3500 feet elevation, increase the flour 2½% and gradually add more as the elevation increases until at 8000 feet elevation 10% more flour is used. For example, if a formula developed at sea level specifies 5 pounds of Softa-silk cake flour (80 oz), use 2 oz more at 3500 feet elevation, making the total 5 lb 2 oz. This amount should be increased as the elevation increases until at 8000 feet elevation 5 lb 8 oz are used.

As mentioned previously, these corrections or adjustments apply particularly to formulas in which the sugar ranges from 120 to 130%, based on flour. In addition, the following recommendations are made for cake baking at altitudes of 4500 feet or over:

1. Grease and dust the cake tins somewhat more thoroughly and heavily, as cakes have a tendency to stick to the sides and bottom of the pans.
2. Beginning at 3500 feet elevation increase the oven temperature approximately 25°F. Keep the baking time the same as for sea level. Precautions should be taken to prevent overbaking because at higher altitudes evaporation takes place much more rapidly, and this will contribute to excess dryness in the baked cake.
3. In formulas specifying either whole eggs, egg whites, or egg yolks, make the altitude adjustments as shown in Figure 3.1 by adding either whole eggs or egg whites. This is recommended to get the benefit of both the egg substance and the extra liquid, which of course is greater in either whole eggs or whites than in the yolks.
4. Less beating of the eggs is required for sponge and angel food cakes, and the acid ingredient (cream of tartar) in the formula should be reduced in the same ratio as for baking powder, as shown in Figure 3.1.
5. Maximum moisture and freshness in the baked cakes can be assured if they are removed from the baking tins as soon as they are taken from the oven. Do not cool freshly baked cakes in a strong current of air. Ice them as soon as possible after they are thoroughly cooled.*

## SCALING WEIGHTS PER CAKE

| Size of Unit | Unit | Scaling Weight | |
|---|---|---|---|
| 6 inches | Layer | | 12 oz |
| 7 inches | Layer | 1 lb | |
| 8 inches | Layer | 1 lb | 8 oz |
| 10 inches | Layer | 2 lb | |
| 12 inches | Layer | 3 lb | |
| 14 inches | Layer | 4 lb | |
| 2¼ × 2½ × 8 inches | Loaf | | 14 oz |

*This data reprinted from the booklet *Quality Cakes,* by permission of General Mills, Inc., copyright owners.

| 17 × 24 inches | Sheet | 5 to 6 lb | |
| 8 inches | Angel | | 13 oz |
| 2¼ × 2½ × 8 inches | Pound loaf | 1 lb | 4 oz |
| 12 oz a dozen | Cupcakes | | 1 oz each |

Note: For American sponge cake, scale all cakes 25% lighter than the above weights.

## CAKE FORMULA CONVERSION TABLE

### Liquids

| | |
|---|---|
| Water | 8 oz = 1 cup |
| Milk | 8½ oz = 1 cup |
| Cream | 8⅜ oz = 1 cup |
| Sweetened condensed milk | 10¼ oz = 1 cup |

### Flours and Fillers

| | |
|---|---|
| Cake flour (sifted once) | 3⅞ oz = 1 cup |
| Bread flour (sifted once) | 4¼ oz = 1 cup |
| Starch (sifted once) | 6½ oz = 1 cup |
| Cake crumbs | 3 oz = 1 cup |

### Sugars

| | |
|---|---|
| Granulated | 7 oz = 1 cup |
| Confectioners' | 5 oz = 1 cup |
| 4X | 4½ oz = 1 cup |
| Brown | 7 oz = 1 cup |
| Fruit fine | 7¾ oz = 1 cup |
| Powdered 6X sifted once | 4 oz = 1 cup |

### Leavenings

| | |
|---|---|
| Baking powder (cream of tartar type) | ⅛ oz = 1 teaspoonful |
| Baking powder (phosphate—S.A.S. type) | ⅙ oz = 1 teaspoonful |
| Cream of tartar | ⅛ oz = 1 teaspoonful |
| Baking soda | ⅙ oz = 1 teaspoonful |

### Flavors

| | |
|---|---|
| Flavoring extracts | ¾ oz = 6 teaspoonfuls |
| Cloves, ground | ½ oz = 6 teaspoonfuls |
| Cinnamon, ground | ½ oz = 6 teaspoonfuls |
| Ginger, ground | ½ oz = 6 teaspoonfuls |
| Mace, ground | ½ oz = 6 teaspoonfuls |

Salt                                              1 oz = 6 teaspoonfuls
Rind, grated                                    ³/₄ oz = 6 teaspoonfuls
Caraway seeds, ground                    ¹/₂ oz = 6 teaspoonfuls


## Shortening

Butter                                          7³/₄ oz = 1 cup
Hydrogenated shortening               6³/₄ oz = 1 cup


## Syrups

Honey                                           12 oz = 1 cup
Molasses                                       11 oz = 1 cup


## Eggs

Whole (approximately)                          5 = 1 cup
Whites (approximately)                         8 = 1 cup
Yolks (approximately)                        12 = 1 cup


## Fruits and Nuts

Coconut, shredded                         3¹/₂ oz = 1 cup
Coconut, ground                            2¹/₂ oz = 1 cup
Nuts, pieces                                      4 oz = 1 cup
Nuts, ground                                 4¹/₄ oz = 1 cup
Applesauce                                        8 oz = 1 cup
Currants                                        4³/₄ oz = 1 cup
Raisins                                          4¹/₂ oz = 1 cup


## Miscellaneous

Candied peel                                      4 oz = 1 cup
Cottage cheese                                  7 oz = 1 cup
Chocolate, scraped                         3³/₄ oz = 1 cup
Chocolate, melted                          8¹/₂ oz = 1 cup
Cocoa                                            3¹/₂ oz = 1 cup
Gelatin                                          5¹/₂ oz = 1 cup

## BUTTER RUM CAKE

| | | |
|---|---|---|
| Sugar | 3 lb | 8 oz |
| Butter | 2 lb | |
| Salt | | 1 oz |
| Vanilla (to taste) | | |
| Eggs | 3 lb | |
| Milk (1 ½ pints) | 1 lb | 8 oz |
| Cake flour | 3 lb | |
| Baking powder | | 1 ½ oz |
| | 13 lb | 2 ½ oz |

*Method:* Creaming. Hold 8 oz of milk and add last.

*Scaling instructions:* 1 lb to a 6-inch ring.

*Baking instructions:* 375°F.

*Syrup:* After baking, remove from pan, cool, and dip in the following rum syrup: Boil together 5 lb of sugar, 1 lb of corn syrup, 1 qt of water, and ½ oz of cream of tartar. Add rum flavor to taste.

## BASIC WHITE CAKE

| | | |
|---|---|---|
| Sugar | 2 lb | 8 oz |
| Cake flour | 2 lb | 8 oz |
| Salt | | 1 oz |
| Baking powder | | 2 oz |
| Vanilla or lemon flavoring (to taste) | | |
| Emulsified shortening | 1 lb | 4 oz |
| Skim milk (1 ½ pints) | 1 lb | 8 oz |
| Egg whites | 1 lb | 8 oz |
| | 9 lb | 7 oz |

*Method:* Two-stage. Hold 8 oz of milk and the egg whites for second stage. Ice with butter cream, chocolate icing, marshmallow icing, etc.

*Scaling instructions:* See table.

*Baking instructions:* 375°F.

CAKES AND TORTES 59

| Ingredients / Main Functions in Finished Products | Binding agent | Absorbing agent | Aids keeping qualities | Affects eating qualities | Nutritional value | Affects flavor | Adds sweetness | Produces tenderness | Affects symmetry | Imparts crust color | Shortness or tenderness | Eating qualities | Color | Volume | Structure | Grain and Texture | Adds quality to product | Brings out flavor |
|---|---|---|---|---|---|---|---|---|---|---|---|---|---|---|---|---|---|---|
| Cake flour | × | × | × | × | × | × | | | | | | | | | | | | |
| Sugar | | | × | | × | | × | × | × | × | | | × | | | | | |
| Shortening and butter | | | × | | × | × | | | | | × | × | | | | | × | |
| Salt | | | | | | | | | | | | | | | | | | × |
| Eggs whole-yolks | | | | | × | × | | | | | | | | | | | | |
| Egg whites | | | | | | | | | × | | | | | × | × | × | | |
| Flavor and spices | | | | | × | | | | | | | | | | | | | × |
| Leavening agent | | | | | | | | | | | | | | × | | × | | |
| Milk | | | × | | | | | | | | | | | | | × | × | × |

Figure 3.2  Cake ingredients and their functions

| Faults \ Causes | Improper mixing | Batter too stiff | Too much leavening agent | Not enough leavening agent | Batter too slack | Too much heat | Not enough heat | Excessive sugar | Not enough sugar | Improper type of flour | Too much flour | Not enough flour | Cakes scaled too light | Aged baking powder | Over-baking | Under-baking | Sugar too coarse | Not enough eggs | Fruit not drained properly | Not enough shortening | Unbalanced formula | Batter too warm | Not enough liquid |
|---|---|---|---|---|---|---|---|---|---|---|---|---|---|---|---|---|---|---|---|---|---|---|---|
| **(External)** | | | | | | | | | | | | | | | | | | | | | | | |
| Crust too dark | | | | | | X | | X | | | | | | | | | | | | | | | |
| Cakes too small | | | | X | | X | | | | X | | | X | X | | | | | | | X | X | |
| Specks on cake | | | | | | | | | | | | | | | | | X | | | | | | X |
| Shrinkage of cakes | X | | | X | | | | | | | | | | | X | | | | | | | | |
| Cake falls during baking | X | | X | | | | | | | | | X | | | | | | | | | | | |
| Cakes burst on top | X | | | | | X | | | | X | X | | | | | | | | | | | | |
| Crust too thick | | | | | X | | | | | | X | | | | | X | | | | | | | |
| Coarse and irregular grain | X | X | X | X | | | X | | | X | | | | | | | | | | | | | |
| Dense grain | | | | | | | | | X | | | | | | | | | X | | | X | | |
| Poor flavor | | X | | | | | | | | | | | | | | | | | | | X | | |
| Cake tough | | X | | | | | | | X | X | | | | | | | | | | | | | X |
| Lack of body in quality | X | | | | | X | | | | | | | | | | | | X | | | | | |
| Sinking of fruit | | X | | | X | | | | | | | | | | | | | | X | | X | | |
| Poor keeping qualities | X | | | | X | | | | | | | | | | | | | X | | X | | | |

Figure 3.3  *Ordinary cake faults and their causes*

# LIGHT FRUITCAKE

| | | |
|---|---|---|
| Raisins | 3 lb | |
| Mixed diced fruit | 3 lb | |
| Cherries | 1 lb | |
| Orange peel | 1 lb | |
| Lemon peel | 1 lb | |
| Citron | 1 lb | |
| Honey | | 13 oz |
| Salt | | 3 oz |
| Ginger | | 1/4 oz |
| Cloves | | 1/4 oz |
| Cinnamon | | 1/4 oz |
| Sherry wine (2 qt) | 4 lb | |
| Sugar | 3 lb | 5 oz |
| Butter and shortening | 2 lb | 6 oz |
| Eggs | 1 lb | 12 oz |
| Bread flour | 4 lb | 2 oz |
| Walnuts | 1 lb | 12 oz |
| | 28 lb | 5 3/4 oz |

*Method:* Soak fruits, peels, and citron overnight in the mixture of honey, salt, spices, and wine. To make the batter, cream together sugar and shortening, cream in eggs, and mix in flour until batter is smooth. Add fruits and walnuts. This mixture may be used for Christmas cake or wedding cake.

*Baking instructions:* 300°–350°F according to size of cake.

# ROMAN APPLE CAKE

| | | |
|---|---|---|
| Sugar | 2 lb | 8 oz |
| Shortening and butter | | 12 oz |
| Salt | | 1/2 oz |
| Mace | | 1/8 oz |
| Cinnamon | | 1/8 oz |
| Eggs | | 8 oz |
| Skim milk (1 pint) | 1 lb | |
| Soda | | 1 oz |
| Cake flour | 2 lb | 10 oz |

| | | |
|---|---|---|
| Baking powder | | 1 oz |
| Apples, chopped | 3 lb | |
| | 10 lb | 8¾ oz |

*Method:* Creaming. Add apples and mix in well.
*Scaling instructions:* 1 lb per 8-inch cake.
*Baking instructions:* 375°F.

*Topping:* Butter 8 oz of pecan nuts with 4 oz of melted butter. Sprinkle nuts over the cake batter and sprinkle cinnamon-sugar mixture over the tops of cakes before baking.

## DATE AND NUT CAKE

| | | |
|---|---|---|
| Cake flour | 2 lb | 8 oz |
| Sugar | 3 lb | |
| Salt | | 1½ oz |
| Soda | | ½ oz |
| Baking powder | | ½ oz |
| Mace | | ⅛ oz |
| Shortening, emulsified | 1 lb | 4 oz |
| Buttermilk (1¼ pint) | 1 lb | 4 oz |
| | | |
| Buttermilk (1¾ pint) | 1 lb | 12 oz |
| Eggs | 1 lb | 8 oz |
| Nuts | 1 lb | |
| Dates, ground | 3 lb | |
| | 15 lb | 6⅝ oz |

*Method:* Two-stage. Add nuts and dates and mix. Ice, preferably with chocolate icing.
*Scaling instructions:* See table of scaling weights.
*Baking instructions:* 375°F.

## AMERICAN SPONGE CAKE

| | | |
|---|---|---|
| Sugar | 6 lb | |
| Eggs, whole | 4 lb | 8 oz |
| Yolks | | 8 oz |
| Vanilla or lemon (to taste) | | |
| Salt | | 1 oz |
| | | |
| Milk (1 1/4 qt) | 2 lb | 8 oz |
| Butter | | 8 oz |
| Cake flour | 4 lb | 8 oz |
| Baking powder | | 2 oz |
| | 18 lb | 11 oz |

*Method:* Heat sugar in a sheet pan. Combine eggs, yolks, salt, and flavoring, and add sugar. Beat to a lemon color, approximately 10 minutes at high speed. Heat milk and butter until butter is melted. Sift flour and baking powder together and blend. Fold into first mixture alternately with milk.

*Scaling instructions:* See chart of scaling weights.

*Baking instructions:* 375°F.

*Variations:* Layer cakes, Boston cream pie, Washington cream pie, ice cream cake, jelly rolls, Mary Ann cups.

## STRAWBERRY LAYER CAKE

| | | |
|---|---|---|
| Cake flour | 3 lb | |
| Sugar | 3 lb | |
| Salt | | 1 1/2 oz |
| Baking powder | | 1 1/2 oz |
| Emulsified shortening | 1 lb | 4 oz |
| Skim milk (1 pint) | 1 lb | |
| | | |
| Eggs | 2 lb | |
| Skim milk (1 pint) | 1 lb | |
| Strawberry paste | 1 lb | 8 oz |
| | 12 lb | 15 oz |

*Figure 3.4 Border designs for cake decoration*

*Method:* Two-stage. Add strawberry paste and mix. Ice with strawberry icing.

*Scaling instructions:* See table of scaling weights.

*Baking instructions:* 375°F.

*Strawberry Paste:* Bring to a boil 2 lb of strawberries and 1 lb of sugar. Cool before using.

## ORANGE AND PINEAPPLE CAKE

| | | |
|---|---|---|
| Cake flour | 1 lb | 4 oz |
| Sugar | 1 lb | 6 oz |
| Baking powder | | 3/4 oz |
| Baking soda | | 1/8 oz |
| Salt | | 1/2 oz |
| Shortening, Hi-ratio | | 8 oz |
| Skim milk | | 8 oz |
| | | |
| Eggs | | 10 oz |
| Skim milk | | 8 oz |
| Orange and pineapple paste | | 10 oz |
| | 5 lb | 7 3/8 oz |

*Method:* Two-stage. Add and mix paste in well.
*Scaling instructions:* See table of scaling weights.
*Baking instructions:* 375°F.

*Orange and pineapple paste:* Bring to a boil 3 lb of ground oranges, 2 lb of pineapple, and 1 lb of sugar. Cool before using. This mixture may be used for pineapple cake, using pineapple paste, or for orange cake, using orange paste. Part of the paste may be used for the filling between layers.

## TORTE DE RICOTTA

| | | |
|---|---|---|
| Ricotta | 1 lb | 8 oz |
| Sugar | | 4 oz |
| Salt | | 1/8 oz |
| Vanilla (to taste) | | |
| Citron (diced fine) | | 1 oz |
| Eggs (4) | | 6 oz |
| Brandy | | 1 oz |
| Toasted almonds | | 4 oz |
| | 2 lb | 8 1/8 oz |

*Method:* Rub ricotta and sugar through fine sieve. Mix salt, vanilla, and citron; add to ricotta and sugar. Gradually add eggs, brandy, and toasted almonds. Make lattice top and bake. Dust with confectioners' sugar. Pour into 8-inch cake pan or 10-inch pie pan lined with cookie dough.
*Baking instructions:* 350°F for about 45 minutes.
*Yield:* 8 to 10 servings (1 pie or cake).

## BAVARIAN CHEESE CAKE

| | | |
|---|---|---|
| Cream Cheese | 6 lb | |
| Granulated Sugar | 2 lb | |
| Brandy | | 6 oz |
| Gelatin | | 2 oz |

*Figure 3.5 Torte de Ricotta; also Bavarian cheese cake*

| Water | 1 cup |
|---|---|
| Salt (to taste) | |
| Lemon rind (to taste) | |
| Orange rind (to taste) | |
| Heavy cream | 5 qt |

*Method:* Bloom gelatin in water. Cream the cream cheese and sugar. Add brandy, salt, lemon, and orange rind. Whip cream and fold into the mixture. Cut ½-inch sponge cake rounds. Place into a 10-inch cake pan and fill with Bavarian cheese cake mixture. Refrigerate. Unmold and top accordingly.

*Yield:* 3-10″ cheesecakes.

## CHEESE CAKE

| | | |
|---|---|---|
| Cream cheese | 10 lb | |
| Sugar | 3 lb | |
| Clear gel | | 8 oz |
| Eggs (20) | 2 lb | |
| Egg yolks (8) | | 6 oz |
| Lemon, vanilla (to taste) | | |
| Heavy cream (1 ¼ pints) | 1 lb | 4 oz |
| | 17 lb | 2 oz |

*Method:* Cream the cream cheese, sugar, clear gel, lemon, and vanilla. Add eggs and egg yolks gradually. Add heavy cream. Divide batter between pans.

*Figure 3.6 Sacher torte*

*Baking instructions: Method 1:* 350°F with water bath for about 1½ hours, just until firm (if overcooked, it will crack while cooling).

*Method 2 (preferred):* 190°F without water bath for 4 hours, just until firm (the protein in the eggs coagulates at 160–180°F; the thickener clear gel sets at 180°F).

*Yield:* 4 10-inch cakes.

## SACHER TORTE

(Created in 1832 by a Viennese pastry cook who worked for Prince Metternich)

| | | |
|---|---:|---:|
| Butter | | 5 oz |
| Sugar | | 3 oz |
| Egg yolks (8) | | 6 oz |
| Sweet chocolate, melted | | 6 oz |
| Egg whites (8) | | 8 oz |
| Granulated sugar | | 2½ oz |
| Cake flour | | 5 oz |
| Clear apricot jam | | 8 oz |
| | 2 lb | 11½ oz |

*Method:* Cream butter and sugar until fluffy; add yolks of eggs two at a time, beating well after each addition. Stir in melted chocolate. Beat egg whites stiff but not dry, adding sugar gradually. Fold into the yolk mixture alternately with the flour, sifted. Pour into a round 10-inch mold, buttered. Bake at 300°F until done. Cool. To finish, slice in half. Fill with apricot or

*Figure 3.7   Black Forest cherry torte*

raspberry filling, spread on top and sides; ice with hard ganache or chocolate fondant. Mark for 16 pieces. For each piece, mark by either writing "Sacher" in chocolate on it or cutting a marzipan circle, writing an S on it in chocolate, and placing a circle on each piece.

## SOFT GANACHE

| | | |
|---|---|---|
| Heavy cream (3 qt) | 6 lb | |
| Milk (1 pint) | 1 lb | |
| Butter | | 8 oz |
| Chocolate, dark sweet, milk, or white | 4½ lb | |
| | 12 lb | |

*Method:* Put milk, cream, and butter in a pot and bring to a boil. Chop the chocolate into small pieces. Pour the boiling milk, cream, and butter over the chocolate and stir with a wooden spoon until smooth. Strain through a china cap, cool at room temperature, and refrigerate.

*Figure 3.8 Mocha torte*

## HARD GANACHE

| | | |
|---|---|---|
| Heavy cream (1 qt) | 2 lb | |
| Sugar | | 2 oz |
| Butter | | 2 oz |
| Chocolate, chopped into small bits | 4 lb | |
| | 6 lb | 4 oz |

*Method:* Boil the cream, sugar, and butter. Pour hot cream mix over chocolate, stir until smooth, and strain.

## ORIGINAL BLACK FOREST CHERRY TORTE

| | | |
|---|---|---|
| 10-Inch chocolate sponge cake | | |
| Fresh black cherries, pitted | 1 lb | |
| Sugar | | 10 oz |
| Cornstarch, diluted | | $^{1}/_{2}$ oz |
| Water | | 5$^{1}/_{3}$ oz |
| Bavarian cream ($^{1}/_{2}$ recipe) | 1 lb | 14 oz |
| Kirsch | | |
| Chocolate shavings | | |
| Whipped cream | | |
| | 3lb | 13$^{5}/_{6}$ oz |

*Method:* Slice cooled cake in three layers. Cook cherries, with sugar. When mixture boils, stir in cornstarch mixed with water. Boil, remove from heat, and cool. Prepare half the recipe of Bavarian Cream. Sprinkle the cake layers with kirsch, and sandwich together with the Bavarian cream and the cooled cherries. Spread sides and top entirely with remaining Bavarian cream. Sprinkle completely with fine chocolate shavings or grated sweet chocolate. Decorate all around with a border of whipped cream. Dust with XXXX sugar. Serve very cold.

*Yield:* 10–12 servings.

# MOCHA TORTE

Slice two layers of vanilla sponge cake and two layers of chocolate sponge cake each ½ inch thick. Fill layers with mocha butter cream or apricot jam in this order: vanilla sponge cake, mocha butter cream, chocolate sponge cake, mocha butter cream, vanilla sponge cake, mocha butter cream, apricot jam, and mocha butter cream. Cover sides and top with mocha butter cream. Make 16 circles of mocha butter cream around top edge of cake. Put apricot jam in each circle. Place sliced toasted almonds in center of cake.

# SPONGE CAKE

| | | |
|---|---|---|
| Eggs (30) | 3 lb | |
| Granulated sugar | 1 lb | 14 oz |
| Cake flour | 1 lb | 6 oz |
| Cornstarch | | 8 oz |
| Butter, melted | | 10 oz |
| Lemon or vanilla (to taste) | | |
| | 7 lb | 6 oz |

*Method:* Whip eggs and sugar to a light foam. Sift flour and cornstarch and fold in. Fold in melted butter last.

*Yield:* 5 10-inch or 8 8-inch cakes.

*Figure 3.9   Chocolate sabayon torte*

## CHOCOLATE SPONGE

| | | |
|---|---|---|
| Eggs (30) | 3 lb | |
| Granulated sugar | 1 lb | 14 oz |
| Cake flour | 1 lb | 1 oz |
| Cocoa powder | | 5 oz |
| Cornstarch | | 8 oz |
| Baking soda (1/2 teaspoon) | | 1/6 oz |
| Butter | | 5 oz |
| Vanilla (to taste) | | |
| | 7 lb | 1 1/6 oz |

*Method:* Whip to a foam eggs and sugar. Fold in by hand sifted flour, cocoa, cornstarch, baking soda, and, last, butter.

## CHOCOLATE SABAYON FILLING

| | | |
|---|---|---|
| Egg yolks (20) | | 14 oz |
| Granulated sugar | | 10 oz |
| Sherry or marsala wine (1 pint) | 1 lb | |
| Sweet chocolate | 1 lb | 4 oz |
| Heavy cream (3 1/2 pints) | 3 lb | 8 oz |
| Vanilla (to taste) | | |
| Brandy (to taste) | | |
| Gelatin | | 1 1/2 oz |
| | 7 lb | 5 1/2 oz |

*Figure 3.10   Linzer torte*

*Method:* Whip egg yolks and sugar. Melt chocolate and add to egg mixture. Whip cream and fold into above. Bloom gelatin in wine.
*Yield:* to fill 5 10-inch cakes.

## CHOCOLATE SABAYON TORTE

Slice three layers of chocolate sponge cake very thin. Sprinkle each with simple syrup. Place one layer in a 10-inch cake pan. Put chocolate sabayon filling on top about half full. Place second layer on top and fill cake pan with remaining chocolate sabayon filling. Place last layer on top and cool in refrigerator. Unmold cake in a water bath, and spread top and sides with chocolate whipped cream. Make 16 rosettes of chocolate whipped cream with No. 5 round tube around tip edge of cake, and place chocolate ornament on each rosette. Cut into 16 pieces.

### Linzer Torte

This native cake from Linz, Austria, is made in many different ways and called by many different names. Some pastry chefs bake three layers of a rich sugar dough mixed with ground almonds. Three small round holes are then cut in the top layer with a small, plain, round cutter.

When baked and cooled, the layers are sandwiched together with raspberry jam. The top layer is glazed with water (flat) icing or simply dusted with XXXX sugar. When this method is used, you are making Linzer krappen.

# LINZER TORTE DOUGH

| | | |
|---|---|---|
| Vegetable shortening | 1 lb | 8 oz |
| Butter | 1 lb | 8 oz |
| Granulated sugar | 1 lb | 8 oz |
| Eggs (5) | | 8 oz |
| Cake flour | 2 lb | |
| Salt | | $1/2$ oz |
| Cinnamon | | $1/4$ oz |
| Fresh cake crumbs | 2 lb | 8 oz |
| Fine-ground walnuts, ha-zelnuts, or almonds | 1 lb | 8 oz |
| | 11 lb | $3/4$ oz |

*Method:* Work shortening, butter, and sugar to a creamy consistency. Add eggs gradually. Sift cake flour, salt, and cinnamon together, and blend with cake crumbs and ground nuts. Fold into mixture, and mix well to produce a smooth dough. Place dough in the refrigerator to cool for at least 2 hours.

*Yield:* 3 10 × 1$1/2$-inch cakes.

# FINISHING LINZER TORTE

Line sides and bottom of a 10 × 1$1/2$-inch cake pan with cold linzer torte dough approximately $3/4$ inch thick. With a flexible spatula, spread a layer of seedless raspberry jam approximately $1/3$ inch thick over the dough in the bottom of the pan. Use a pastry bag filled with linzer torte dough and fitted with a plain $3/4$-inch tube to squeeze a lattice pattern over the jam. Brush with beaten eggs; sprinkle with sliced almonds. Bake at 375°F for 35–40 minutes or until done. When cool, dust with XXXX sugar.

## OPEN FRUIT TORTEN

### Tart Shell

Grease a tart mold 10 inches in diameter and 1$1/2$ inches deep. Line with 1-2-3 dough. Form a thick, rounded rim of dough around the inside circumference of the mold. Flute the edges evenly; pinch with pastry pinchers and

*Figure 3.11   Apple torte maison*

prick the bottom with a fork. Place a greased paper over the dough and fill it with beans or rice to prevent the dough from rising. Bake in a 400°F oven for about 30 minutes. Empty out rice or beans, remove paper, and return to over for approximately 15 minutes or until shell starts to color. Prebaked tart shells can be baked in advance and stored for a few days in a dry place.

### Finishing

Line the bottom of baked tart shells with a ³/₄-inch layer of pastry cream flavored with kirsch, rum, or liqueur. Cover with a thin layer of sponge cake, and arrange drained canned or fresh fruit on top. Glaze with red currant jelly or apricot glaze. If desired, garnish with whipped cream. Canned apricots, peaches, cherries, pears, or pineapple or fresh strawberries, blueberries, or other fruits used freely make attractive combinations in garnishing.

### Optional Method for Finishing

Line a greased tart mold 10 inches in diameter and 1½ inch deep with 1-2-3 dough or puff paste dough. Flute the edges evenly and pinch with pastry pinchers. Pour a ½-inch layer of pastry cream or Franchipan in the bottom of the mold. Cover with a thin layer of sponge cake, and arrange fruits attractively and as close to each other as possible because fruit will shrink during baking. Fresh, firm fruits such as apples, cherries, and pears are ideal; if canned fruit is used, the juice must be thoroughly drained. Bake in a 400°F oven for approximately 1 hour. Cool. Unmold and glaze with apricot jam or red currant jelly.

# FRANCHIPAN I. (for fillings)

| | | |
|---|---|---|
| Almond paste | 4 lb | |
| Butter | 2 lb | |
| Granulated sugar | | 6 oz |
| Eggs (16) | 1 lb | 10 oz |
| Cake flour | | 6 oz |
| | 8 lb | 6 oz |

*Method:* Mix and soften almond paste. Add butter and mix smooth. Add sugar. Mix and add eggs in 3 parts. Add flour and mix smooth.

### French Apple Torte

Line a 10 × 1½-inch mold with 1-2-3 dough. Fold the rim and flute evenly. Spread the bottom with ½-inch layer of vanilla pastry cream. Cover with a very thin slice of sponge cake and sprinkle lightly with rum. Peel, core, and slice ⅛ inch thick 8 large baking apples. Place the apples over the sponge cake in circular rows, close together, until the pan is well covered (fresh apples shrink during baking). Sprinkle the torte with granulated sugar. Bake at 400°F for 45 minutes or until done. To help the apples bake through, cover the torte with a buttered paper halfway during the baking process.

### Apple Torte Maison

Line a 10 × 1½-inch mold with 1-2-3 dough. Spread a little apricot jam in the bottom, and cover with one row of fresh apples sliced ¼ inch thick. Stir together 1 pint milk, 1 egg yolk, 3 eggs, 6 oz sugar, and 1 oz cornstarch. Pour over the fresh apples to within ⅔ of the mold's capacity. Bake at 400°F for 40 minutes. Cool for 30 minutes before unmolding.

*Figure 3.12   Dobos torte*

## 1 - 2 - 3   D O U G H   ( C O O K I E )   D O U G H

| | | |
|---|---|---|
| Granulated sugar | 1 lb | |
| Butter | 2 lb | |
| Eggs (3) | | 5 oz |
| Flavor | | |
| Cake flour | 3 lb | |
| | 6 lb | 5 oz |

*Method:* Cream sugar and butter. Add eggs and flavor. Add sifted cake flour.

## DOBOS TORTE

This very rich and delectable cake is originally from Budapest. This torte is loved all over the world for its taste and its unusual presentation.

## D O B O S   T O R T E   M I X

| | | |
|---|---|---|
| Egg yolks (10) | | 7 oz |
| Granulated sugar | | 6 oz |
| Heavy cream (1/3 cup) | | 3 oz |
| Bread flour | | 8 oz |
| Egg whites (10) | | 10 oz |
| | 2 lb | 2 oz |

*Method:* Beat egg yolks and sugar together until thick. Gradually add heavy cream, and stir well to blend all ingredients. Add bread flour, sifted. Mix thoroughly, and fold in stiffly beaten egg whites.

### Preparing and Finishing Dobos Torte

Butter heavily the bottoms of 7 12-inch layer cake tins (or use spring-form molds). With a flexible spatula, spread with a thin layer of dobos torte mix. Bake at 400°F for 10–12 minutes or until done. Sandwich 6 layers together with a rich chocolate butter cream or ganache. Ice the remaining layer with caramel sugar with a spatula, and cut immediately into 12 equal pieces with a buttered knife. Mask the cake entirely with chocolate butter cream, and place on top the caramel sugar triangles. A little dot of chocolate butter cream under each will help to make it stand up.

In some cases the dobos torte top is simply coated with melted couverture of sweet chocolate. Spread dobos torte mix over 18 × 24-inch baking sheet pans, and sandwich together with chocolate butter cream. Cut in long, narrow strips and ice with couverture.

### Caramel Sugar

Melt 1 cup granulated sugar and 1 tablespoon butter in a saucepan. Stir over a low fire until mixture starts to brown.

## BAVARIAN CREAM TORTE

Slice 3 layers of sponge cake very thin. Sprinkle each with simple syrup. Place a layer in a 10-inch cake pan. Put Bavarian cream filling on top about half full. Place second layer on top and fill cake with remaining filling. Place last layer on top and refrigerate. Unmold cake in a water bath and spread sides and top with vanilla-flavored whipped cream. Make 16 whipped cream rosettes with star tube around top edge of cake, and decorate with fresh fruit such as mandarin oranges, cherries, or strawberries.

*Figure 3.13   Bavarian cream torte*

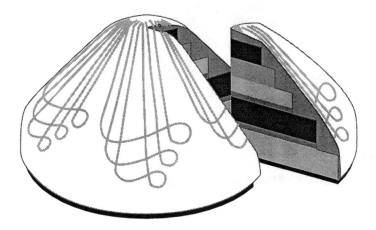

*Figure 3.14   Marzipan torte*

## MARZIPAN TORTE

This torte is a combination of vanilla and chocolate sponge cake; strawberry, chocolate, and vanilla whipped cream; fresh strawberries or other fresh fruit, and light green pistachio marzipan. Layer as follows: vanilla sponge cake, strawberry whipped cream, chocolate sponge cake, chocolate whipped cream, vanilla sponge cake, vanilla whipped cream, fruit, and chocolate sponge cake. Cover cake with 1/8-inch layer of pistachio marzipan, and decorate with piping gel.

VANILLA WHIPPED CREAM

CHOCOLATE CAKE

VANILLA SPONGE CAKE

WHIPPED CREAM

MARZIPAN

VANILLA SPONGE CAKE

CHOCOLATE CAKE

STRAWBERRY WHIPPED CREAM

*Figure 3.15   Marzipan, whipped cream, chocolate cake, vanilla whipped cream, vanilla sponge cake, chocolate cake, chocolate cake, strawberry whipped cream, vanilla sponge cake*

*Figure 3.16*

*Figure 3.17   Fruit torte*

## FRUIT TORTE

This torte could be made in many different ways as long as it looks like a
very elegant open fruit pie. Choose from the following possibilities:

| | |
|---|---|
| First layer | Franchipan |
| | 1-2-3 dough |
| | Linzer dough |
| | |
| Jam | Raspberry |
| | Strawberry |
| | Apricot |
| | |
| Cake | Sponge cake |
| | High-ratio cake |
| | Pound cake |
| | |
| Icing | Pastry cream |
| | Whipped cream |
| | Chantilly cream |
| | |
| Fruit | Mandarin oranges |
| | Pineapple |
| | Strawberries |
| | Raspberries |

## FLUFFY CHEESE CAKE

| | | |
|---|---|---|
| Baker's cheese | 4 lb | |
| Cake flour | | 4 oz |
| Cornstarch | | 8 oz |
| Salt | | 2 oz |
| Vanilla (to taste) | | |
| Soft butter | | 8 oz |
| Eggs | 2 lb | |
| Milk (1 pint) | 1 lb | |
| Egg whites | 1 lb | 8 oz |
| Cream of tartar | | 1/2 oz |
| Sugar | 2 lb | |
| Water (1/2 pint) | | 8 oz |
| | 12 lb | 6 1/2 oz |

*Method:* Mix cheese, flour, cornstarch, salt, vanilla, and butter until smooth. Blend eggs and milk, add, and mix until smooth. Beat egg whites until stiff, as for meringue. Boil sugar, water, and cream of tartar to 240°F. Add to beaten whites and make into a stiff meringue. Then fold into cheese mixture.

*Baking instructions:* 300°F. Grease cake pans and sprinkle with cake crumbs. Fill with the above mixture about seven-eighths full.

## CHEESE CAKE

| | | |
|---|---|---|
| Baker's cheese or cream cheese | 2 lb | 8 oz |
| Sugar | 1 lb | 4 oz |
| Salt | | 1/4 oz |
| Milk solids | | 3 oz |
| Bread flour | | 1 1/2 oz |
| Shortening, emulsified | | 8 oz |
| Eggs, whole | | 8 oz |
| Yolks | | 4 oz |
| Water (1 pint) | 1 lb | |
| | 6 lb | 4 3/4 oz |

*Method:* Mix until smooth cheese, sugar, salt, milk solids, and bread flour. Add shortening, eggs, and yolks, and mix until smooth. Add water; the amount will vary according to the dryness of the cheese.

*Scaling instructions:* 2 lb per 8-inch cake.

*Baking instructions:* 350°F. Line 8-inch cake pans with sugar cookie dough. Fill pans full with above mixture. Dust lightly with powdered cinnamon. Pie filling, such as cherry or pineapple, may be used on the bottom of the pan before placing cheese filling in the pan. Bake until filling is set. Take care not to overbake.

## BRIDE'S CAKE

| | | |
|---|---|---|
| Sugar | 4 lb | |
| Butter and shortening | 1 lb | 2 oz |
| Vanilla (to taste) | | |
| Salt | | 1 oz |
| Egg whites | 2 lb | |
| Milk | 3 lb | |
| Cake flour | 4 lb | |
| Baking powder | | 2 oz |
| | 14 lb | 5 oz |

*Method:* Creaming.

*Baking instructions:* Fill pans two-thirds full and bake at 325°F.

## MACAROON CUPCAKES

| | | |
|---|---|---|
| Egg whites | 2 lb | |
| Salt | | $^1/_2$ oz |
| Vanilla (to taste) | | |
| Cream of tartar | | $^1/_4$ oz |
| Sugar | 1 lb | 8 oz |
| Sugar | 2 lb | |
| Cake flour | | 3 oz |
| Macaroon coconut | 2 lb | 8 oz |
| | 8 lb | $3^3/_4$ oz |

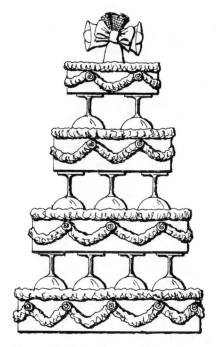

*Figure 3.18   Tiered wedding cake with champagne glass dividers*

*Method:* Whip egg whites, salt, and vanilla until foamy. Add sugar and cream of tartar and continue to whip until whites peak. Blend sugar, flour, and coconut and fold into mixture.

*Scaling instructions:* 8 dozen cupcakes.

*Baking instructions:* Fill cupcake forms 7/8 full and bake at 375°F.

## DEVIL FUDGE CAKE

| | | |
|---|---|---|
| Cake flour | 2 lb | |
| Cocoa | | 8 oz |
| Sugar | 3 lb | 8 oz |
| Salt | | 1 1/2 oz |
| Baking powder | | 1 1/2 oz |
| Cinnamon | | 1/8 oz |
| Baking soda | | 1/2 oz |
| Shortening, emulsified | 1 lb | |
| Skim milk (1 1/4 pints) | 1 lb | 4 oz |
| | | |
| Skim milk (1 1/2 pints) | 1 lb | 8 oz |
| Eggs | 1 lb | 8 oz |
| | 11 lb | 7 5/8 oz |

*Method:* Two-stage. Ice with devil fudge icing.
*Scaling instructions:* See table of scaling weights.
*Baking instructions:* 375°F.

## BANANA CAKE

| | | |
|---|---|---|
| Cake flour | 2 lb | 8 oz |
| Sugar | 3 lb | |
| Salt | | 1 1/2 oz |
| Baking powder | | 1 1/2 oz |
| Baking soda | | 1/2 oz |
| Shortening, emulsified | 1 lb | |
| Bananas, ripe | 2 lb | |
| Skim milk (1 pint) | 1 lb | |
| Eggs | 2 lb | |
| Vanilla (to taste) | | |
| | 11 lb | 11 1/2 oz |

*Method:* Mix dry ingredients, shortening, bananas, and milk 5 to 7 minutes at slow speed. Add eggs and vanilla in three parts, scraping sides of bowl each time, and mix 3 to 5 minutes. Ice with banana icing.

*Scaling instructions:* See table of scaling weights.
*Baking instructions:* 375°F.

# JELLY ROLL SPONGE

| | | |
|---|---|---|
| Eggs, whole | | 12 oz |
| Yolks | | 6 oz |
| Sugar | 1 lb | 8 oz |
| Salt | | 1/2 oz |
| Vanilla or lemon (to taste) | | |
| Milk powder | | 1 1/2 oz |
| Water | | 12 oz |
| Honey | | 3 oz |
| Cake flour | 1 lb | 5 oz |
| Baking powder | | 1/2 oz |
| | 5 lb | 1/2 oz |

*Method:* Beat eggs, yolks, sugar, salt, vanilla, and milk powder for approximately 10 minutes at high speed until the mixture becomes lemon colored. Heat honey and water and add to first mixture. Sift together flour and baking powder and fold in.

*Scaling instructions:* Line two 18 × 24-inch sheet pans with paper, and divide dough between them.

*Baking instructions:* 375°F.

*Variations:* Jelly roll, lemon roll, mocha roll, marshmallow roll, ice cream roll.

*Chocolate Roll:* Use 1 lb of cake flour, 5 oz of cocoa, and 1/2 oz of baking soda. Proceed the same way.

# FRENCH COFFEE CAKE

| | | |
|---|---|---|
| Sugar | 2 lb | 4 oz |
| Shortening and butter | 1 lb | 2 oz |
| Salt | | 1/2 oz |
| Vanilla (to taste) | | |
| Eggs | 1 lb | 8 oz |
| Milk (1 qt) | 2 lb | |
| Cake flour | 3 lb | |
| Baking powder | | 1 1/2 oz |
| | 10 lb | |

*Method:* Creaming. Top cake with streusel before baking. After baking, cool and cut into 2-inch squares and serve.
*Scaling instructions:* 18 × 24 × 1-inch sheet pans.
*Baking instructions:* 375°F.

# YELLOW CAKE, BASIC

| | | |
|---|---|---|
| Cake flour | 5 lb | |
| Sugar | 5 lb | |
| Salt | | 3 oz |
| Baking powder | | 3 3/4 oz |
| Shortening, emulsified | 2 lb | 6 oz |
| Skim milk (1 qt) | 2 lb | |
| Eggs | 2 lb | 8 oz |
| | | |
| Skim milk (1 1/2 pints) | 1 lb | 8 oz |
| Vanilla (to taste) | | |
| | 18 lb | 12 3/4 oz |

*Method:* Two-stage.
*Scaling instructions:* See table of scaling weights.
*Baking instructions:* 350°–375°F.

*Variations:* sheet cake, loaf cake, cupcakes, layer cakes.

# CHOCOLATE CAKE

| | | |
|---|---|---|
| Sugar | 2 lb | 8 oz |
| Shortening and butter | 1 lb | |
| Cake flour | 2 lb | |
| Salt | | $3/4$ oz |
| Baking powder | | $3/4$ oz |
| Baking soda | | $1/4$ oz |
| Vanilla (to taste) | | |
| Bitter chocolate, melted | | 8 oz |
| Skim milk (1$1/4$ pints) | 1 lb | 4 oz |
| | | |
| Eggs | 1 lb | 4 oz |
| Skim milk ($3/4$ pint) | | 12 oz |
| | 9 lb | 5$3/4$ oz |

*Method:* Two-stage. Ice with chocolate icing.
*Scaling instructions:* See table of scaling weights.
*Baking instructions:* 375°F.

# APPLE SAUCE CAKE

| | | |
|---|---|---|
| Cake flour | 2 lb | 8 oz |
| Sugar | 2 lb | 8 oz |
| Baking powder | | 1 oz |
| Baking soda | | $1/2$ oz |
| Cinnamon | | $1/4$ oz |
| Cloves | | $1/4$ oz |
| Salt | | 1$1/2$ oz |
| Shortening, emulsified | 1 lb | |
| Applesauce | 3 lb | |
| Eggs | | 12 oz |
| Raisins | 1 lb | 8 oz |
| | 11 lb | 7$1/2$ oz |

*Method:* Mix together for 5 to 7 minutes at slow speed flour, sugar, baking
soda, baking powder, spices, salt, shortening, and half of the applesauce.

Add eggs. Add remaining applesauce and raisins, scraping sides of bowl. Mix 3 to 5 minutes at slow speed. Add raisins last. Ice with lemon icing.

*Scaling instructions:* See table of scaling weights.

*Baking instructions:* 375°F.

## GINGERBREAD CAKE

| | | |
|---|---|---|
| Sugar | 2 lb | 8 oz |
| Shortening, Hi-ratio | 1 lb | 4 oz |
| Eggs | 1 lb | 4 oz |
| Molasses | 4 lb | |
| Cake flour | 5 lb | |
| Baking soda | | 3½ oz |
| Cinnamon | | 1 oz |
| Ginger | | 1 oz |
| Salt | | 2 oz |
| Skim milk (2 qt) | 4lb | |
| | 18 lb | 7½ oz |

*Method:* Cream sugar and shortening. Add eggs and cream. Stir in molasses. Sift and blend together dry ingredients, add milk, and mix smooth.

*Scaling instructions:* See table of scaling weights.

*Baking instructions:* 360° to 375°F.

*Variations:* layer cakes, sheet cakes, Mary Ann cups.

## ANGEL FOOD CAKE

| | | |
|---|---|---|
| Egg whites | 2 lb | |
| Vanilla (to taste) | | |
| Sugar | 1 lb | |
| Cream of tartar | | ¼ oz |
| Salt | | ¼ oz |
| | | |
| Sugar | 1 lb | |
| Cake flour | | 13 oz |
| | 4 lb | 13½ oz |

*Method:* Beat egg whites and vanilla at high speed for 5 minutes. Blend sugar, cream of tartar, and slowly add egg whites, beating until they form a wet peak. Sift flour and blend with sugar, add, and fold in. Precautions should be taken not to overbeat this mixture and to fold in flour and sugar only after whites are thoroughly mixed. Otherwise, the cakes will collapse and the volume will be smaller.

*Baking instructions:* 350°F. Turn the cake upside down after removing from the oven. Allow to cool before removing from pans.

## YELLOW POUND CAKE

| | | |
|---|---|---|
| Cake flour | 5 lb | |
| Sugar | 5 lb | |
| Baking powder | | 1 oz |
| Salt | | 2 oz |
| Nutmeg | | 1/4 oz |
| Shortening, emulsified | 2 lb | |
| Butter | 1 lb | |
| Skim milk (1 qt) | 2 lb | |
| Eggs | 3 lb | |
| Milk (1 pint) | 1 lb | |
| Vanilla (to taste) | | |
| | 19 lb | 3 1/4 oz |

*Method:* Two-stage.
*Scaling instructions:* See table of scaling weights.
*Baking instructions:* 350°F.

*Variations:* raisin pound cake, nut fudge cake, marble pound cake.

## OLD-FASHIONED PLAIN POUND CAKE

| | | |
|---|---|---|
| Fine granulated sugar | 2 lb | |
| Butter | 2 lb | |
| Whole eggs (20) | 2 lb | |
| Vanilla or almond flavor (1 teaspoon) | | ⅓ oz |
| Cake flour sifted with ½ oz Baking powder | 2 lb | |
| | 8 lb | ⅚ oz |

*Method:* Cream sugar and butter well; gradually add eggs two by two. Add flavoring and flour sifted with baking powder.

*Baking instructions:* 325°F for 50–75 minutes.

*Yield:* three loaf cakes, 3 lb, 6 oz each.


## CHIFFON CAKES

Chiffon cakes are first cousins to the well-known angel food cake. Like the angel food variety, they should be baked immediately after mixing (egg whites have a tendency to drop rapidly if exposed to the air too long). When cool, they can be spread with the icing or frosting of your choice.

A high-grade liquid vegetable oil such as the type used in salad dressings is essential. Melted butter or plastic fats (hydrogenated shortenings) do not perform satisfactorily.

Be careful not to overmix or excessively aerate the first part of the batter. Whip egg whites until they are firm and stand in a stiff peak. Egg whites must be firmer than for angel food, but not dry. Add the batter mixture in a steady stream to the beaten egg whites as fast as the whites will take it. Mix only enough to thoroughly blend the two together.

Scale batter immediately into small center tube, 10-inch, 13-egg angel food pans (4 inches deep). Place in oven immediately and bake 45 to 50 minutes. (handle same as angel food, turning cakes upside down immediately after removal from oven).

*Yield:* Cakes scaled at 1 lb 12 oz each.

# VANILLA CHIFFON CAKE

| | | |
|---|---|---|
| Cake flour | 1 lb | 12 oz |
| Baking powder | | 1 1/4 oz |
| Salt | | 3/4 oz |
| Granulated sugar | 1 lb | 8 oz |
| Vegetable Oil | | 14 oz |
| Egg yolks (20) | | 14 oz |
| Water | 1 lb | 5 oz |
| Vanilla flavor | | Few drops |
| Egg whites | 1 lb | 12 oz |
| Granulated sugar | | 12 oz |
| Cream of tartar | | 1/4 oz |
| | 8 lb | 15 1/4 oz |

*Method:* Sift flour, baking powder, salt, and sugar into a mixing bowl. Using a paddle at moderate speed, add the vegetable oil, egg yolks, and water in several portions. Do not overmix. In a separate bowl, beat egg whites stiff, adding the sugar and cream of tartar gradually. Fold beaten egg whites into the batter with the help of a flat skimmer until all ingredients are well blended.

*Scaling instructions:* 10 × 4-inch center-tube pan at 1 lb 14 oz each.

*Baking instructions:* 350°F for 45–50 minutes. Handle like angel food cake.

*Yield:* 4–5 cakes.

## C O C O A   C H I F F O N   C A K E

| | | |
|---|---|---|
| Cake flour | 1 lb | 8 oz |
| Cocoa | | 3 oz |
| Salt | | 3/4 oz |
| Baking powder | | 1 1/4 oz |
| Granulated sugar | 1 lb | 10 oz |
| Egg yolks (26) | 1 lb | 2 oz |
| Vegetable oil | | 14 oz |
| Water | 1 lb | 6 oz |
| Vanilla flavor | | 1/2 oz |
| Egg whites (28) | 1 lb | 12 oz |
| Granulated sugar | | 10 oz |
| Cream of tartar | | 1/4 oz |
| | 9 lb | 3 3/4 oz |

*Method:* Sift cake flour, cocoa, salt, and baking powder together into a mixing bowl along with the granulated sugar. Using medium speed and paddle, add yolks, vegetable oil, water, and vanilla gradually. Beat egg whites to soft peak. Add sugar and cream of tartar and beat stiff. Fold batter into the beaten egg whites gradually. Scale batter in 10-inch center-tube pans.

*Baking instructions:* 350°F for 45–50 minutes. Handle like angel food cake.

*Yield:* 5 cakes.

## SHEET CAKES

The simplest form of pastry dessert that can be made is the sheet cake. It is simple because it can be made from a variety of baking mixes, all of them available from a food wholesaler. On the package of these mixes are simple, one-two-three steps for mixing and baking sheet cakes. The sheet cake can also be made from a recipe. In either case, the sheet cake becomes a base that offers a variety of opportunities. It is not only easy to make but also easy to decorate to fit any occasion.

For instance, in school lunch programs, the sheet cake can be used as a good, plain, and inexpensive food, or it can be frosted and trimmed to delight youngsters. In a restaurant, the same sheet cake becomes the basis of tiny decorative petit fours. Variations run from the plain and simple to the formal and extra-fancy desserts. The variety comes in the trim.

One of the many advantages of the sheet cake is its ability to stay fresh.

Baked as one large unit, the sheet cake retains its moisture and freshness much longer than many smaller units that are more fully exposed to the air and therefore more readily dry out.

This staying quality is especially important. It offers volume feeders an opportunity to take advantage of slack kitchen time and use it creatively and profitably. The cakes can be baked ahead and stored. This also guarantees not getting caught short when the need for pastry and cake arises unexpectedly.

## CUTTING CAKES

There is a satisfactory method of cutting each kind of cake. The factors to keep in mind are the size and number of servings and the cutting utensil to be used. The size and number of servings depend upon the size and number of layers in the cake. A knife with a sharp, straight-edged, thin blade is most suitable for cutting batter cakes. To make a clean cut, dip the blade into warm water before cutting each portion and keep the blade free from frosting and cake crumbs.

Fruit cake, which also is a batter-type cake, may be cut in the same manner. Because of its richness, fruit cake servings generally are smaller than those shown for layer cakes.

The accompanying diagrams illustrate methods of cutting cakes of various sizes and shapes. The average number of servings per cake are given.

## BUNDER NUSS TORTE

This popular dessert comes from St. Moritz, the well-known winter resort.

Roll out sugar cookie dough approximately 1/8 inch thick and line a greased 10 × 1-inch round cake pan. Fill 3/4 full with franchipan cream. Bake at 400°F for 30–35 minutes or until done. Cool and unmold. Meanwhile, prepare the following topping:

Figure 3.19   Sheet cake cutting chart

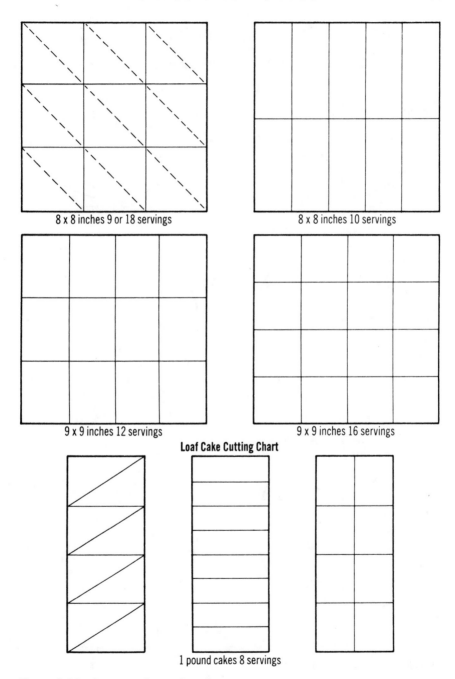

8 x 8 inches 9 or 18 servings

8 x 8 inches 10 servings

9 x 9 inches 12 servings

9 x 9 inches 16 servings

**Loaf Cake Cutting Chart**

1 pound cakes 8 servings

*Figure 3.20 Square cake cutting chart*

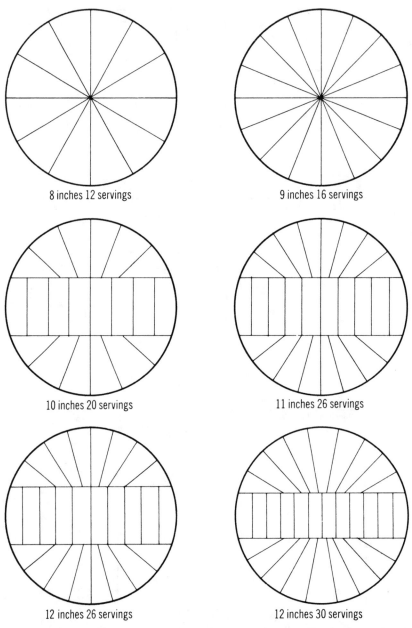

8 inches 12 servings

9 inches 16 servings

10 inches 20 servings

11 inches 26 servings

12 inches 26 servings

12 inches 30 servings

Three-layer cakes should be cut in the same manner as shown above. However, reduce the size of each serving approximately one-third in order to increase the number of servings.

*Figure 3.21   Two-layer cake cutting chart*

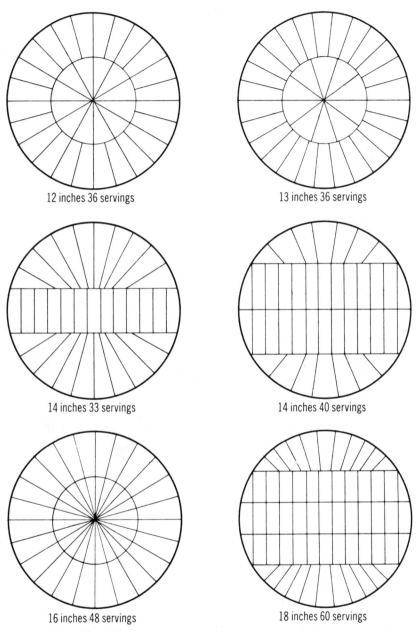

12 inches 36 servings

13 inches 36 servings

14 inches 33 servings

14 inches 40 servings

16 inches 48 servings

18 inches 60 servings

Three-layer cakes should be cut in the same manner as shown above. However, reduce the size of each serving approximately one-third in order to increase the number of servings.

*Figure 3.22  Two-layer cake cutting chart*

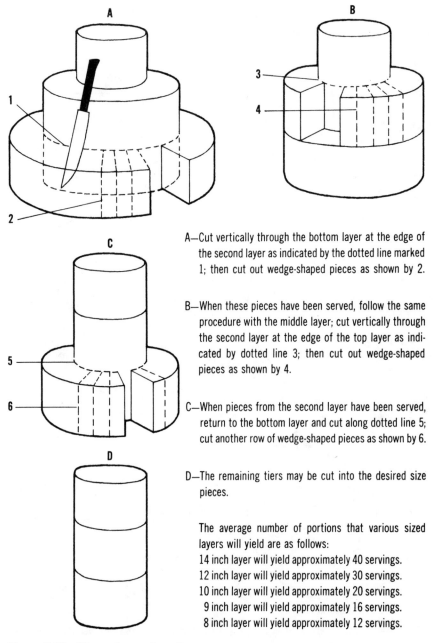

A—Cut vertically through the bottom layer at the edge of the second layer as indicated by the dotted line marked 1; then cut out wedge-shaped pieces as shown by 2.

B—When these pieces have been served, follow the same procedure with the middle layer; cut vertically through the second layer at the edge of the top layer as indicated by dotted line 3; then cut out wedge-shaped pieces as shown by 4.

C—When pieces from the second layer have been served, return to the bottom layer and cut along dotted line 5; cut another row of wedge-shaped pieces as shown by 6.

D—The remaining tiers may be cut into the desired size pieces.

The average number of portions that various sized layers will yield are as follows:
14 inch layer will yield approximately 40 servings.
12 inch layer will yield approximately 30 servings.
10 inch layer will yield approximately 20 servings.
 9 inch layer will yield approximately 16 servings.
 8 inch layer will yield approximately 12 servings.

*Figure 3.23   Tier cake cutting chart*

*Figure 3.24   Zuger-kirsch torte*

## BUNDER NUSS TORTE TOPPING

| | | |
|---|---|---|
| Sugar | | 6 oz |
| White corn syrup | | 1 oz |
| Butter | | 3 oz |
| Heavy cream, scalded (¹/₃ cup) | | 3 oz |
| Walnuts or pecans, halved | | 6 oz |
| | 1 lb | 3 oz |

*Method:* Place sugar and corn syrup in a saucepan. Cook, stirring constantly to ensure an even melting and coloring to golden caramel. Remove from heat. Stir in butter. Heat cream. Add butter to caramel mixture; return to a slow fire for 1 minute or so until butter is completely dissolved.

Remove from heat; add scalded heavy cream. Fold in the nuts. Blend all ingredients well. Cool to lukewarm. Spread topping, (using a slightly oiled flexible spatula), over the baked and cooled franchipan cream. Chill in the refrigerator for approximately 30 minutes before serving. This amount of topping is sufficient for 2 10-inch cakes.

## ZUGER KIRSCH TORTE

The origin of the Zuger kirsch torte can be traced to the village of Zug, in Switzerland, a country well known for its hospitality.

To prepare it, butter and flour a regular baking sheet pan. With the help of a knife and a cake pan, draw 2 10-inch circles. Prepare japonais meringue and, with a pastry bag fitted with a plain ¹/₄-inch tube, fill up each circle, starting from the center and going around until a complete layer is made, or simply spread the meringue mixture evenly about ¼ inch thick with a flexible spatula. Bake both layers at 310°F until done. Remove from pan while still warm, and cool thoroughly.

From a 10-inch sponge cake, cut a layer approximately 1½ inches thick. Sprinkle both sides with plain syrup diluted with an equal amount of kirsch.

Flavor 1½ pints of vanilla butter cream with 4 oz of kirsch, and add a few drops of red coloring; blend all ingredients well. Butter cream should now be light pink. Spread some butter cream over japonais bottom; place sponge cake over it, and spread more butter cream on top. Secure remaining japonais layer over the top of the sponge cake, and press gently to sandwich the prepared sponge layer properly. Mask sides entirely with butter cream. Sprinkle with roasted sliced almonds. Dust the top with XXXX sugar, and mark the top in a lattice pattern, using the point of a knife. Refrigerate for at least 2 hours before serving. Yield: 10 to 12 servings.

# JAPONAIS

| | |
|---|---|
| Egg whites (16) | 1 lb |
| Granulated sugar | 2 lb |
| Filberts | 1 lb |
| | 4 lb |

*Method:* Follow instructions for making a meringue with sugar and egg whites. Fold in finely granulated filberts by hand.

*Baking instructions:* 250°F.

## GATEAU ST. HONORÉ

Roll out sugar cookie dough or 1-2-3 dough approximately ¼ inch thick, and cut a 10-inch circle. Prick well. Place on lightly buttered pan. Make a rim around the edge with cream puff paste using a pastry bag and a plain round ⅝-inch tube. Brush the rim with beaten eggs, and bake at 400°F for 35 minutes or until done. Drop about 12 small puffs the size of a ping-pong ball, and bake at 350°F for 30 minutes, or until done. Cool; fill each puff with vanilla pastry cream. Dip each puff in hot caramel sugar; arrange puffs close together on top of the cream puff ring. Fill the center with cream for St. Honoré.

*Figure 3.25  Gateau Saint Honoré*

Note: To obtain a thicker coating, cool the caramel sugar slightly before dipping the puff.

## CREAM FOR ST. HONORÉ

| | | |
|---|---|---|
| Unflavored gelatin | | ³⁄4 oz |
| Boiling water | | 8 oz |
| Egg yolks (8) | | 6 oz |
| Sugar | | 5 oz |
| Milk (1 pint) | 1 lb | |
| Cornstarch | | 1 oz |
| Egg whites beaten stiff (10) | | 10 oz |
| Sugar | | 3 oz |
| | 3 lb | 1³⁄4 oz |

*Method:* Soak gelatin in water. Work yolks and sugar together until thick. Bring milk to a boil. Add cornstarch to egg mixture, and blend well. Pour boiling milk over the yolk mixture gradually, and stir rapidly, mixing all ingredients thoroughly. Return to the fire and boil 1–2 minutes. Add gelatin and stir well. Fold beaten egg whites immediately into the hot cream. Flavor with vanilla.

*Figure 3.26    Pithivers*

## PITHIVIERS

Roll out a round piece of puff paste about ½ inch thick. Fill with franchipan cream 1 inch thick, not too close to the edge. Cover with a piece of puff paste ¼ inch thick, but of the same diameter as the first. Cut both circles evenly with a knife or a cutter. Press all around the edge with your fingers to join both circles of dough securely. Mark the sides with the back of a knife, and with the point, starting from the center, mark the top of the dough with curve lines. Wash with beaten eggs. Let rest 2 hours in a cool place, and bake at 425°F to start for 15 minutes. Cover with heavily buttered paper, and finish baking. Before baking is completed, sprinkle with XXXX sugar, and return to a hot oven to glaze.

## FRUIT CONDÉ

| | | |
|---|---|---|
| Milk (1 pint) | 1 lb | |
| Blanched rice | 1 lb | |
| Salt | | ¼ oz |
| Sugar | | 4 oz |
| Gelatin, unflavored | | ½ oz |
| Heavy cream, whipped | 1 lb | |
| Nesselrode mixture | | 6 oz |
| | 3 lb | 10¾ oz |

*Method:* Place milk, blanched rice, salt, sugar, and gelatin in a pot and simmer for 10 minutes. Allow to cool and set. Whip cream and fold into mixture that has set. Add Nesselrode mixture. Place this mixture in a large or small charlotte mold. Refrigerate until mixture is set. Unmold on a dish;

*Figure 3.27   Fruit Condé*

place assorted fruit on top of rice mixture. Brush top of fruit with a hot apricot sauce and serve.

*Variations:* Strawberry condé, peach condé, apricot condé, pineapple condé; for rice imperative, use raspberry gelatin on bottom of mold. Allow to set and add condé mixture.

# C O O K I E S

Cookies are one of the most profitable items produced by bakers. Important in their production is the use of high-grade ingredients. Butter is the preferred shortening. Careful choice of the purest of spices, molasses, and flavorings will assure delicious cookies. Cookies should be baked fresh each day, if possible. When it is necessary to bake a week's output at one time, this can be done if the cookies are properly stored.

## MIXING METHODS

There are two basic methods for mixing cookies: the creaming method and the one-stage method.

### Creaming Method

1. Place the sugar, butter or shortening, salt, and spices in a mixing bowl and cream together.
2. Add the eggs and liquid.
3. Add the flour and leavening agent last.

### One-Stage Method

1. Place all ingredients into a mixing bowl and mix until all are smoothly blended.
2. Allow two or three minutes at low speed for mixing.

## TYPES OF COOKIES

There are six basic kinds of cookies: rolled, icebox, spritz, bar, sheet, and dropped.

*Rolled Method:* The dough is easier to handle if chilled first. Roll out 1/8-inch thick on a flour bag. Cut to desired shape and size with a cookie cutter. Place on baking sheets and bake.

*Icebox Method:* Weigh dough at 1 lb 8 oz and roll into bars 18 inches long. Roll in waxed paper and place rolls on sheet pans. Refrigerate overnight. Slice into 1/2-inch strips and bake.

*Spritz or Bagged Method:* Put mixture into pastry bag with desired size and shape tube. Press directly onto sheet pans. Garnish with cherries, nuts, etc., and bake.

*Bar Method:* Scale the dough into 1-lb pieces and roll out to the length of the sheet pan. Place on the sheet pans, leaving a space between the strips. Place three strips on each pan. Flatten with the fingers and shape into uniform 1-inch strips. Apply egg wash and bake.

*Sheet Method:* Spread the cookie mixture onto sheet pans. Wash with egg or sprinkle with nuts and bake. Cool and cut into squares or oblongs.

*Dropped Method:* Drop mixture on sheet pans with a spoon. Press or flatten out with a weight or special cookie die. Strips of dough may also be cut into 1/2-inch pieces. If the dough is rich, it will spread by itself. Do not press or flatten.

## THE PASTRY BAG

The pastry bag of yesterday was generally made of canvas. Today the pastry bag is made of a specialized material, nonabsorbing, durable, and easy to clean. It has many uses. Its contents may range from mashed potatoes to elegant cream mixtures. Its uses in the kitchen are unlimited: duchess potatoes, fancy mashed potato borders on various meat, fish, or vegetable platters; fancy cookies; garnishes and toppings of various mixtures; fancy cream toppings. The pastry bag is used to fill pastries, and last but not least, the pastry bag is filled with icings to decorate the simplest or fanciest cakes.

To care for the pastry bag, one fact is very important—it must always be turned inside out and scrubbed very thoroughly after each use, using hot water. This will prevent the bag from becoming sour and stale after being filled with the rich mixtures. Remember to always remove the tube when

*Figure 4.1   The pastry bag*

washing the pastry bag; the tube must also be carefully washed and stored. To dry the pastry bag, hang it up by the loop to enable it to air dry.

The pastry bag comes with various pastry tubes of different shapes and sizes. Select the one you want and insert it into the bag from the inside. To

| Faults \ Causes | Improper mix | Insufficient sugar | Too much sugar | Flour too strong | Too much flour | Insufficient leavening | Too much leavening | Too much baking soda | Not enough baking soda | Insufficient eggs | Too much shortening | Insufficient shortening | Over-baked | Too low baking temperature | Too high baking temperature | Pan insufficiently greased | Dough too slack | Insufficient liquid | Poor quality ingredients | Unbalanced formula | Cookie pans unclean and uneven |
|---|---|---|---|---|---|---|---|---|---|---|---|---|---|---|---|---|---|---|---|---|---|
| Spreading | × |  | × |  |  |  |  | × |  |  |  |  |  | × |  |  | × |  |  |  |  |
| Crumbly | × |  | × |  |  |  | × |  |  | × | × |  |  |  |  |  |  |  |  |  |  |
| Tough | × | × | × | × | × |  |  |  |  |  |  |  |  |  |  |  |  |  |  |  |  |
| Hard |  |  |  | × | × |  |  |  |  |  |  | × | × | × |  |  |  | × |  |  |  |
| Dry |  |  |  | × | × |  |  |  |  |  |  | × | × | × |  |  |  | × |  |  |  |
| Pale in color |  | × |  |  | × |  | × |  |  |  |  |  |  | × |  |  |  |  |  | × |  |
| Lack of flavor |  |  |  |  |  |  |  |  |  |  |  |  |  |  |  |  |  |  | × | × | × |
| Sticking to pans | × |  | × |  |  |  |  |  |  |  |  |  |  |  |  | × |  |  |  |  | × |
| Sugary crust | × | × |  |  |  |  | × |  |  |  |  |  |  |  |  |  |  |  |  |  |  |
| Lack of spread | × | × |  | × |  | × |  |  | × |  |  |  |  |  | × | × |  |  |  |  |  |

Figure 4.2  Ordinary cookie faults and their causes

fill the pastry bag, fold back half of the bag, and hold it open with the left hand under the fold. Place the mixture into the bag with the right hand, using a spatula or spoon. Fill no more than two-thirds full. Close up the bag and give a slight twist at the top to seal off the mixture and eliminate leakage from the top.

To use the bag, squeeze from the top with the right hand, and guide with the left, leaving the tube visible. When using a stiff mixture, hold the top of the bag closed with the left hand and squeeze the lower section of it with the right hand. This method requires less pressure.

## PECAN COOKIES OR PECAN DIAMONDS

This prize-winning cookie recipe is outstanding.

| | | |
|---|---|---|
| Sugar dough | 3 lb | 8 oz |
| Butter | 1 lb | |
| Honey | | 12 oz |
| Granulated sugar | | 4 oz |
| Brown sugar | 1 lb | |
| Pecan pieces | 2 lb | |
| Heavy cream (1/2 cup) | | 4 oz |
| | 8 lb | 12 oz |

*Method:* Line the bottom and sides of a greased 18 × 24-inch baking sheet with sugar dough. Prick. Bake at 425°F for 15 minutes or until dough is half baked. Place butter cut in pieces, honey, and sugars in a deep saucepan and boil all ingredients for 3 minutes. Remove from heat, stir in pecans and heavy cream, and, using a wooden spoon or a flexible spatula, immediately spread the hot mixture evenly over the half-baked sugar dough.

*Baking instructions:* 400°F for 35–40 minutes. Cool and cut in 1 1/2-inch squares or diamond shapes. Yields approximately 300 cookies.

## ICEBOX COOKIES (Yellow Mix)

| | | |
|---|---|---|
| Confectioners' sugar | 2 lb | |
| Butter and shortening | 2 lb | |
| Salt | | ½ oz |
| Vanilla (to taste) | | |
| Eggs | | 8 oz |
| Cake flour | 3 lb | |
| | 7 lb | 8½ oz |

*Method:* Creaming. Roll into strips about 18 inches long. Roll a piece of waxed paper around each strip. Pack the strips on sheet pans. Place in refrigerator overnight. Remove from refrigerator and slice into ¼-inch slices. A slicing machine may be used to assure uniformity. Place on ungreased pans. Bake lightly, avoiding too much bottom heat.

*Scaling instructions:* Each strip, 1 lb 8 oz.

*Baking instructions:* 375°F.

*Variations:* Fruit or nuts may be added to this mix. Checkerboard and pinwheels can be made from yellow mix and chocolate mix.

## ICEBOX COOKIES (Butterscotch)

| | | |
|---|---|---|
| Brown sugar | 1 lb | |
| Confectioners' sugar | 1 lb | |
| Butter | 1 lb | 8 oz |
| Salt | | ½ oz |
| Eggs, whole | | 10 oz |
| Cake flour | 3 lb | |
| Baking powder | | ¼ oz |
| | 7 lb | 2¾ oz |

*Method:* Follow same instructions as for icebox cookies *(yellow mix).*

*Baking instructions:* 375°F.

## I C E B O X   C O O K I E S   ( W h i t e   M i x )

| Confectioners' sugar | 2 lb | |
| Butter and shortening | 2 lb | |
| Salt | | ¹/₂ oz |
| Almond flavoring (to taste) | | |
| Egg whites | | 8 oz |
| Cake flour | 2 lb | 12 oz |
| | 7 lb | 4¹/₂ oz |

*Method:* Follow same instructions as for icebox cookies *(yellow mix).*
*Scaling instructions:* 8 oz per roll.
*Baking instructions:* 375°F.

## I C E B O X   C O O K I E S   ( C h o c o l a t e )

| Confectioners' sugar | 1 lb | 12 oz |
| Butter and shortening | 1 lb | 8 oz |
| Salt | | ¹/₂ oz |
| Vanilla (to taste) | | |
| Eggs, whole | | 12 oz |
| Milk | | 4 oz |
| Soda | | ¹/₈ oz |
| Cake flour | 3 lb | |
| Cocoa | | 8 oz |
| | 7 lb | 12⁵/₈ oz |

*Method:* Follow same instructions as for icebox cookies *(yellow mix).*
*Baking instructions:* 375°F.

## CHOCOLATE BROWNIES

| Bittersweet chocolate | 1 lb | |
|---|---|---|
| Butter | 1 lb | 8 oz |
| Eggs | 1 lb | 4 oz |
| Sugar | 3 lb | |
| Vanilla (to taste) | | |
| Cake flour | 1 lb | |
| Nuts (pecans or walnuts) | 1 lb | 8 oz |
| | 9 lb | 4 oz |

*Method:* Melt chocolate and butter. Beat together eggs, sugar, and vanilla until lemon colored (about 10 minutes). Add chocolate and butter. Sift flour and fold into mixture. Add only enough flour to incorporate well. Fold about 1 lb of nuts into the mixture. Place mixture into sheet pan. Sprinkle balance of nuts on top of mixture.

*Scaling instructions:* 9 lb 4 oz per 18 × 24-inch sheet pan. The yield is about 8 doz 2 × 2-inch brownies; cut 8 × 12 to each sheet pan.

*Baking instructions:* 350°F.

## BUTTERSCOTCH BROWNIES

| Brown sugar | 2 lb | |
|---|---|---|
| Butter | 1 lb | |
| Water | | 4 oz |
| Eggs | 1 lb | |
| Brown sugar | 1 lb | |
| Vanilla (to taste) | | |
| Baking powder | | ½ oz |
| Cake flour | 2 lb | |
| Walnuts | 1 lb | 8 oz |
| | 8 lb | 12½ oz |

*Method:* To make butterscotch mixture, dissolve sugar, butter, and water with heat. Beat eggs, sugar, and vanilla until lemon colored (about 10 minutes) and add to butterscotch. Sift flour and baking powder and fold into mixture. Add 1 lb of nuts and mix. Place in an 18 × 24-inch sheet pan and sprinkle top with 8 oz of chopped nuts.

*Scaling instructions:* 8 lb 12 oz per 18 × 24-inch sheet pan. Yields about 8 doz 2 × 2-inch brownies. Cut 8 × 12 to each sheet pan.
*Baking instructions:* 325°F.

## BROWNIES (One-stage method)

| | | |
|---|---|---|
| Whole eggs | 1 lb | 10 oz |
| Granulated sugar | 4 lb | 8 oz |
| Shortening | 1 lb | |
| Butter | 1 lb | 8 oz |
| Cocoa | 1 lb | |
| Glucose | 1 lb | 10 oz |
| Cold water | | 8 oz |
| Cake flour | 3 lb | 2 oz |
| Salt | | 1 oz |
| Chopped pecans | 3 lb | |
| | 17 lb | 15 oz |

*Method:* Scale all ingredients into the mixing bowl, and mix at medium speed to a smooth dough. Spread on greased and floured pans.
*Baking instructions:* 400°F. Yields 3 18×24-inch sheet pans of 324 brownies.

## FANCY BUTTER COOKIES

| | | |
|---|---|---|
| Almond paste | | 8 oz |
| Powdered sugar | 1 lb | 8 oz |
| Eggs | 1 lb | |
| Shortening and butter | 2 lb | |
| Cake flour | 3 lb | |
| | 8 lb | |

*Method:* Rub together almond paste and sugar. Add eggs gradually to obtain a smooth batter. Add shortening and whip until light. Add flour and mix until smooth. Do not overmix. Then tube out to form various shapes.
*Baking instructions:* 375°F.

# VANILLA WAFERS

| | | |
|---|---|---|
| Sugar | 1 lb | |
| Butter and shortening | 1 lb | |
| Salt | | 1/4 oz |
| Vanilla (to taste) | | |
| Eggs | | 12 oz |
| Pastry flour | 1 lb | 6 oz |
| | 4 lb | 2 1/4 oz |

*Method:* Creaming. Bag out with plain tube on slightly greased pans. Leave sufficient space between drops for spreading. Bake until the edges are brown; remove from oven. Avoid overbaking.

*Baking instructions:* 375°F.

# FRENCH MACAROONS

| | |
|---|---|
| Almond and macaroon paste | 2 lb |
| Powdered sugar | 12 oz |
| Granulated sugar | 12 oz |
| Egg whites* | 8 oz |
| | 4 lb |

*Method:* Break up paste and sugars until fine. Gradually add whites until a smooth medium paste is obtained. Bag out with fine star tube on paper-lined pans. Decorate with fruit or nuts, let stand overnight, and bake on double pans in a hot oven. Glaze while still hot with a hot mixture of three parts glucose and one part water.

*Baking instructions:* 400°F.

*Egg whites vary depending on the dryness of the paste.

## COCONUT MACAROONS (Chewy)

| | | |
|---|---|---|
| Sugar | 1 lb | |
| Water | | 4 oz |
| Glucose | | 4 oz |
| Butter | | 2 oz |
| Salt | | 1/8 oz |
| Vanilla (to taste) | | |
| Macaroon (coconut) | 1 lb | |
| Cake flour | | 1 oz |
| Cream of tartar | | 1/8 oz |
| Egg whites | | 6 oz |
| | 3 lb | 1 1/4 oz |

*Method:* Bring sugar, water, glucose, butter, salt, and vanilla to a boil. Remove from heat and mix in rest of ingredients. Bag out with plain tube on paper-lined sheet pans.

*Baking instructions:* 325°–350°F.

## COCONUT MACAROONS
## (Light Meringue)

| | | |
|---|---|---|
| Sugar | 1 lb | |
| Water | | 4 oz |
| Egg whites | | 8 oz |
| Granulated sugar | | 8 oz |
| Salt | | 1/4 oz |
| Vanilla (to taste) | | |
| Macaroon (coconut) | 1 lb | |
| | 3 lb | 4 1/4 oz |

*Method:* Boil sugar and water to 242°F to make syrup. Whip egg whites and vanilla until light and add sugar until a wet peak is produced. Then add syrup. Bag out on paper-lined pans with star tube.

*Baking instructions:* 300°F.

## ALMOND MACAROONS

| | | |
|---|---|---|
| Almond paste | 2 lb | |
| Granulated sugar | 2 lb | |
| Egg whites (variable) | | 10 oz |
| | 4 lb | 10 oz |

*Method:* Rub paste and sugar together until fine. Add whites gradually to sugar and paste until smooth. This makes a medium stiff paste. Press out with a plain tube on paper-lined sheet pans. Dampen the macaroons with a towel before baking. Do not permit them to dry before placing in the oven.
*Baking instructions:* 325°F.

## CHOCOLATE CHIP COOKIES

| | | |
|---|---|---|
| Brown and granulated sugar | 1 lb | 8 oz |
| Butter and shortening | 1 lb | 8 oz |
| Baking soda | | 1/2 oz |
| Salt | | 1/2 oz |
| Water | | 1 oz |
| Vanilla (to taste) | | |
| Eggs | | 8 oz |
| Pastry flour | 2 lb | 4 oz |
| Chocolate chips | 1 lb | |
| Walnuts, chopped | | 8 oz |
| | 7 lb | 6 oz |

*Method:* Creaming. Bag out with plain tube on slightly greased pans.
*Baking instructions:* 375°F.

## SHORTBREAD COOKIES (Sables)

| | | |
|---|---|---|
| Sugar | | 14 oz |
| Butter | 1 lb | 8 oz |
| Salt | | 1/2 oz |
| Lemon rind (1 lemon) | | |
| Egg yolks | | 8 oz |
| Cake flour | 2 lb | |
| | 4 lb | 14 1/2 oz |

*Method:* Creaming. Refrigerate for several hours. Roll out about 1/4-inch thick and cut into various shapes. Wash and sprinkle with nuts or granulated sugar or decorate with nuts or cherries.
*Baking instructions:* 350°F.

## SHORT PASTE COOKIE DOUGH

| | | |
|---|---|---|
| Sugar | 1 lb | |
| Shortening and butter | 1 lb | 8 oz |
| Salt | | 1/2 oz |
| Eggs | | 4 oz |
| Milk | | 4 oz |
| Vanilla (to taste) | | |
| Pastry flour | 2 lb | 8 oz |
| | 5 lb | 8 1/2 oz |

*Method:* Creaming. Roll out about 1/8-inch thick and cut out with cookie cutters into various shapes. Wash and decorate. Bake lightly.
*Baking instructions:* 375°F.

## RAINBOW SLICE COOKIES

| | | |
|---|---|---|
| Granulated sugar | 3 lb | |
| Shortening and butter | 3 lb | |
| Salt | | 1 oz |
| Vanilla (to taste) | | |
| Lemon flavoring (to taste) | | |
| Eggs | 4 lb | |
| Cake flour | 4 lb | |
| Baking powder | | 1 oz |
| | 14 lb | 2 oz |

*Method:* Creaming. Divide entire mixture into 4 equal parts. Color each part separately—green, yellow, pink, and orange. Spread each mixture on paper-lined sheet pans. Bake lightly. When cool, spread jam lightly over cake, sandwiching all 4 colored layers. Press down well with sheet pan, making an even, firm sandwich. Roll out marzipan 1/16-inch thick and place on the upper side of cake. Melt sweet chocolate and spread over marzipan. Allow to set. Reverse sheet, placing marzipan layer on the other side, and spread with melted chocolate. Cut into 1½-inch by ½-inch slices when dry.

*Baking instructions:* 375°F.

## GINGERSNAPS

| | | |
|---|---|---|
| Brown sugar | | 12 oz |
| Shortening | 1 lb | |
| Salt | | ½ oz |
| Water | | 4 oz |
| Baking soda | | ½ oz |
| Molasses (1 pint) | 1 lb | 2 oz |
| Pastry flour | 2 lb | |
| Ginger | | ½ oz |
| | 5 lb | 3½ oz |

*Method:* Cream together sugar, salt, and shortening. Dissolve baking soda in water and add to first mixture. Stir in molasses. Sift flour and ginger together and mix with above until smooth. Refrigerate for several hours. Roll out 1/8-inch thick and cut out with cutters.

*Baking instructions:* 375°F.

*Variations:* This mixture may also be used for gingerbread houses and for gingerbread men.

## NUT WAFERS—NUT FINGERS

| | | |
|---|---|---|
| Egg whites | 1 lb | |
| Sugar | 1 lb | |
| Confectioners' sugar | 1 lb | |
| Nuts, finely sifted | 1 lb | |
| Cornstarch | | 2 oz |
| Cinnamon (to taste) | | |
| | 4 lb | 2 oz |

*Method:* Beat egg whites and add sugar until a wet peak meringue is secured. Blend remaining ingredients and fold into egg whites. Bag out with a plain tube onto paper-lined pans. Press out round or in finger shapes.

*Baking instructions:* 275°F.

## PEANUT BUTTER COOKIES

| | | |
|---|---|---|
| Brown and granulated sugar | 2 lb | |
| Shortening | 1 lb | |
| Peanut butter | 1 lb | 8 oz |
| Salt | | 1/2 oz |
| Eggs | 1 lb | |
| Milk | | 4 oz |
| Baking soda | | 1/4 oz |
| Pastry flour | 2 lb | |
| Baking powder | | 1/4 oz |
| | 7 lb | 13 oz |

*Method:* Cream together sugar, shortening, peanut butter, and salt. Add eggs and cream together. Dissolve baking soda in milk and add. Sift together flour and baking powder, add to mixture, and mix until smooth. Roll into strips, flatten, and wash. After baking, cut out while still warm.

*Scaling instructions:* 96 cookies.

*Baking instructions:* 350°F.

## SUGAR COOKIES

| | | |
|---|---|---|
| Sugar | 1 lb | |
| Shortening | | 12 oz |
| Salt | | 1/2 oz |
| Eggs | | 6 oz |
| Milk | | 6 oz |
| Vanilla (to taste) | | |
| Pastry flour | 2 lb | |
| Baking powder | | 1/4 oz |
| | 4 lb | 8 3/4 oz |

*Method:* Cream together sugar, shortening, and salt. Add eggs and cream. Stir in milk and vanilla. Sift together flour and baking powder, add to mixture, and mix until smooth. Roll out 1/4-inch thick and sprinkle granulated sugar over the surface. Cut out and bake on lightly greased pans.

*Baking instructions:* 375°F.

## BUTTER COOKIES

| | | |
|---|---|---|
| Sugar | 1 lb | |
| Butter | 1 lb | |
| Salt | | 1/4 oz |
| Eggs | | 8 oz |
| Pastry flour | 2 lb | |
| | 4 lb | 8 1/4 oz |

*Method:* Creaming. Roll out 1/8-inch thick and cut out with various shaped cookie cutters—stars, bells, rabbits, animal figures, etc. Wash, decorate, and bake.

*Baking instructions:* 375°F.

# LADYFINGERS

| | |
|---|---|
| Egg whites, 16 | 1 lb |
| Sugar | 1 lb |
| Egg yolks, 16 | 1 lb |
| Bread flour | 1 lb |
| | 4 lb |

*Method:* Gradually add sugar to whites, and beat to a stiff peak. Beat yolks and fold into mixture. Sift flour and fold into mixture. Press into finger shapes with a plain tube on paper-lined sheet pans. Dust with powdered sugar and bake immediately.

*Baking instructions:* 400°F.

# OATMEAL COOKIES

| | | |
|---|---|---|
| Sugar | 1 lb | |
| Shortening | | 8 oz |
| Salt | | 1/2 oz |
| Malt and molasses | | 8 oz |
| Eggs | | 4 oz |
| Milk | | 8 oz |
| Baking soda | | 1/2 oz |
| Pastry flour | 1 lb | 4 oz |
| Baking powder | | 3/4 oz |
| Oatmeal | | 12 oz |
| Raisins | 1 lb | |
| | 5 lb | 13 3/4 oz |

*Method:* Cream together salt, sugar, shortening, malt, and molasses. Add eggs. Dissolve baking soda in milk and stir in. Add flour, oatmeal, and raisins, and mix thoroughly. Bag out with a plain tube onto lightly greased pans.

*Baking instructions:* 375°F.

# **MINTS**

| Sugar | 3 lb | |
| Water (1 pint) | 1 lb | |
| Peppermint flavor (to taste) | | |
| Confectioners' sugar | 1 lb | 8 oz |
| | 5 lb | 8 oz |

*Method:* Cook sugar and water to a soft ball, 238°–240°F. After cooking, add flavoring and confectioners' sugar and mix smooth. Pipe out onto paper, marble slab, or rubber mat.

## PETIT FOURS

Petit fours (or, as they are known in America, tea cakes or small fancy cakes), may be classified into two categories: petit fours glacé and petit fours sec.

*Petit fours glacé* are generally very small (petit) fancy cakes made from various sponges, cake mixtures, and franchipan (see recipe below); sometimes they are left with no filling and sometimes they are filled with jams, icing, cream, or marzipan. They are made in many different shapes and iced or glazed with colored fondant, chocolate, or jellies. Then they are decorated with fancy designs—florals or abstract designs, for instance. Petit fours make for good eating and also have a great deal of eye appeal.

To make petit fours glacé use a firm type of sponge or yellow cake one-half inch in thickness. Remove the sheet cake from the pan and trim off all loose crust. Spread surface with hot apricot jam. Next, cut small dainty squares, oblongs, or diamond shapes and arrange these pieces carefully on the icing screen. Then with your pastry tube filled with prepared butter cream, pipe out an oval bulb of buttercream onto each piece. Place these in the refrigerator to chill thoroughly. Remove them from refrigerator and ice with fondant icing in a variety of colors. When dry, set in paper cases and decorate with appropriate designs.

*Petit fours sec* (or dry type) are small fancy cakes or cookies made from cookie dough, almost paste, or marzipan and combined with jams, icings, creams, chocolate, and the like. Unlike petit fours glacé, petit fours sec are not coated with fondant. Fancy cookies are also sometimes classified as petit fours sec. It must be remembered that petit fours sec must be made very carefully and patiently for best results.

*Figure 4.3   Petit fours glacé*

*Figure 4.4   Petit fours sec*

# FRANCHIPAN II.

| | | |
|---|---|---|
| Butter | | 8 oz |
| Sugar | | 8 oz |
| Almond paste | 1 lb | |
| Eggs | | 4 oz |
| | | |
| Eggs | | 8 oz |
| Bread flour | | 5 oz |
| | 3 lb | 1 oz |

*Method:* Cream together butter and sugar. Soften almond paste with eggs and add to butter and sugar. Continue to cream this mixture. Add remaining eggs and cream well. Add flour, mix smooth, and pan as required.

*Baking instructions:* 375°F.


## CHINESE ALMOND COOKIES

| | | |
|---|---|---|
| Cake flour | 1 lb | |
| Sugar | | 8 oz |
| Baking soda | | 1/4 oz |
| Baking powder | | 1/4 oz |
| Shortening | | 8 oz |
| Eggs, whole (2 large) | | 4 oz |
| Almond extract (to taste) | | |
| | 2 lb | 4 1/4 oz |

*Method:* Sift together dry ingredients and blend. Add shortening and mix. Add remaining ingredients and mix. Brush cookies with milk and place a split almond on top.

*Scaling instructions:* 1 oz per cookie.

*Baking instructions:* 375°F.


## CHOCOLATE LEAVES

| | | |
|---|---|---|
| Almond paste | 1 lb | |
| Confectioners' sugar | | 12 oz |
| Bread flour | | 4 oz |
| Egg whites | | 4 oz |
| Milk (variable) | | 4 oz |
| | 2 lb | 8 oz |

*Method:* Rub together almond paste, sugar, and flour, and blend thoroughly. Add egg whites and mix smooth. Add and mix milk into proper consistency. Bake on greased and floured pans. Cover with melted chocolate after baking and mark to give leaf effect.

*Baking instructions:* 350°F.

# CHAPTER FIVE

# PIES

## PIE CRUSTS

There are two basic types of pie crusts: flaky pie crust and mealy pie crust. Although they may contain identical ingredients in the same amounts, the results may be quite different.

*Flaky crust* is made by rubbing the flour and shortening together until they become nuggets the size of walnuts before adding the liquid and salt.

*Mealy crust* is made by rubbing the flour and shortening together until there is a finer distribution of the shortening through the flour.

### Ingredients

Always use a soft wheat flour, such as pastry flour, for pie crusts. If a stronger flour is used, it must be worked with a higher proportion of fat. Shortening used in making pie crusts must be of plastic consistency. Lard is a good choice but many people object to the taste. Vegetable shortening is most popular. A proportion of butter greatly improves the flavor and should be used where the cost factor is not too serious. Water must always be very cold when used for making pie crusts. The salt is usually dissolved in the water.

Thus the essential ingredients that go into the making of a good pie crust are pastry flour, vegetable shortening (with some butter added if possible), salt, and cold water. Some formulas may call for other ingredients such as vinegar or baking powder, but these items do not improve the crust.

One important point: pie dough should never be overmixed.

*Pie trimmings:* When crusts are being rolled out, care should be taken to keep the size of each piece as near as possible to the size of the pans, thus keeping the size of the trimmings to a minimum. Pie trimmings should be used to make no more than half of a crust and should be used for the bottom crust only.

*Pie washes:* Milk, cream, eggs and milk, melted butter, and water are the various kinds of pie washes used to improve eye appeal of pie crusts. The wash to be used depends upon the finish required.


## PIE FILLINGS

There are five main types of pie fillings.

1. Fruit pie. The most popular fruit pies are apple, cherry, blueberry, and rhubarb. The fruit used may be fresh, frozen, canned, dried, or prepared pie filling.
2. Cream pie.
3. Chiffon pie.
4. Soft pie.
5. Specialty pies.

### Fruit Pie Filling Preparation

Among the many methods used in filling pies today, the following are the most generally accepted.

*Cooked Juice Method:* Drain the juice from fruit and bring to a boil. Thicken with the proper amount of dissolved cornstarch. Bring back to a boil to clarify and ensure the proper setting of the starch. Add granulated sugar, salt, spices, butter, or other flavoring agents and stir until dissolved. Pour over the drained fruit and stir carefully so as not to crush or mash the fruit. When the filling is cold, it is ready for the pies. This method is generally used for cherry, apple, blueberry, apricot, and peach pies.

*Cooked Fruit and Juice Method:* Bring juice and fruit to a boil. Add the amount of dissolved cornstarch needed to bring the juice and fruit to the proper consistency. After the cornstarch is added, always bring the filling back to a boil so that it will clarify. Add the desired amount of sugar and stir until thoroughly dissolved. Care should be taken when cooking the fruit to stir occasionally to prevent scorching. When the filling is cold, it is ready for

*Figure 5.1   Lattice pie top*

the pies. This method is generally used for raisin, pineapple, and apple pies if the latter are unusually hard.

*Homemade Method:* Mix the fruit with spices, flour, and sugar. Fill the unbaked pie shells. Place a lump of butter or margarine on top of the filling. Cover the pie and bake as usual. This method is very simple. However, the flour in the filling has a tendency to remain uncooked, and the consistency is not as easily controlled as in the preceding two methods.

## Cream Pie Filling

Vanilla, chocolate, butterscotch, banana, and coconut are the most popular cream pies.

Care should be taken to acquire a good smooth cream with a delicate flavor. This cream filling is always placed into prebaked pie shells.

*Cream Pie Method:* Place the milk with part of the sugar in a round-bottomed pan and scald. Mix the egg yolks, balance of sugar, starch, and flour into a paste. Add part of milk to make mix into liquid form. When the first part is near the boiling point, add the egg mixture and continue to stir until the filling comes to a boil. Remove from heat. Add the necessary flavoring to this mixture and stir. Place in prebaked pie shells. After cooling, top with meringue or whipped cream.

## Chiffon Pie Filling

Chiffon pies are mixed similarly to the cooked fruit and juice method under fruit filling or the cream pie method. Meringue is folded into this mixture. Both cream pies and fruit pies may be converted into chiffon pies.

*Chiffon Pie Method:* Place in a pan the fruit, sugar, flavoring, coloring, salt, and water or milk. Bring to a boil on top of the stove. Dissolve the starch in juice or water, mix with the first part, and continue to boil. Remove from heat. Make meringue with egg whites and sugar. Fold the meringue into the above mixture *immediately* while it is still hot. Place the mixture into a prebaked pie shell. Remember to fill the shell generously, pyramiding it into the shell with a spatula. Allow pie to cool and top with whipped cream.

## Soft and Specialty Pies

Pumpkin, sweet potato, squash, custard, and pecan pies are known as "soft" pies. They require a deep pie plate with an additional fluted pie crust rim.

Soft pies are made with an unbaked crust and uncooked filling. The filling is "set" during the baking process as it contains eggs, which help in the coagulation.

Each one of the soft pies is made in accordance with a specific formula developed in the following pages.

Nesselrode, ice cream, and Boston cream pies are known as "specialty" pies. They are made by a combination of the foregoing methods and are developed from formulas in the following pages.

### Thickening agents

Starches and flour are used as thickening agents in pie fillings. Starches are used more often because they do not have a tendency to discolor and become gummy.

The amount used depends upon the jelling quality of the starch, the amount of liquid in the filling, and the desired consistency of the finished pie. Approximately 2 to 5 ounces of cornstarch for each quart of liquid (juice plus water) are used in the preparation of different fillings.

## PIE CRUST (for general use)

| | | |
|---|---|---|
| Pastry flour | 3 lb | |
| Shortening | 2 lb | |
| Salt | | 1 oz |
| Cold water or milk (1 pint) | 1 lb | |
| | 6 lb | 1 oz |

*Method:* Rub shortening into flour to form nuggets the size of walnuts. Dissolve salt in liquid. Add and mix with flour and shortening.
*Baking instructions:* 400°–425°F.

## GRAHAM CRACKER CRUST

| | | |
|---|---|---|
| Graham crackers, ground | 1 lb | |
| Butter, melted | | 6 oz |
| Sugar | | 6 oz |
| | 1 lb | 12 oz |

*Method:* Mix crumbs and sugar. Add melted butter. Rub with your hands until it has a wet, sandy consistency. Pour crumb mixture into 9-inch pie plate. Set 8-inch pie plate on top of crumbs and press firmly to make an even layer of crumbs. Crust shell is now ready to fill and use as is, to freeze for ice cream pie, or to bake in 375°F oven for 8 minutes to obtain a crisper crust and extra flavor. (Makes approximately four 9-inch pie crusts.)

| Faults | Overmixed | Insufficient shortening | Too much shortening | Improperly mixed | Insufficient liquid | Too much liquid | Improper flour | Overworking of dough | Baking temperature too low | Baking temperature too high | No bottom oven heat | Excess acidity in filling | Hot filling used | Lack of opening on top crust | Improperly sealed crusts | Filling too thin | Wet pie plates | Boiling over of filling | Too much sugar | Insufficient sugar | Watery egg whites | Not beaten firm enough |
|---|---|---|---|---|---|---|---|---|---|---|---|---|---|---|---|---|---|---|---|---|---|---|
| **Pie dough** | | | | | | | | | | | | | | | | | | | | | | |
| Stiff | X | X | | | X | | | | | | | | | | | | | | | | | |
| Crumbly | X | | X | | X | | | | | | | | | | | | | | | | | |
| Tough | X | X | | | | X | X | | | | | | | | | | | | | | | |
| **Baked crust** | | | | | | | | | | | | | | | | | | | | | | |
| Shrinkage | X | X | | | | X | X | X | | | | | | | | | | | | | | |
| Solid crust | | X | | | | X | X | X | | | | | | | | | | | | | | |
| Too light in color | | | | | | | | | X | | | | | | | | | | | | | |
| Tough | X | X | | | | X | X | X | | | | | | | | | | | | | | |
| **Two-crust pies** | | | | | | | | | | | | | | | | | | | | | | |
| Unbaked crust bottom | | | | | | | | | X | | X | | | | | | X | | | | | |
| Boiling of filling during baking | | | | | | | | | X | | | X | X | X | X | | | | X | | | |
| Crust sticking to pans | | X | | | | | | | | X | X | | | | | | X | X | | | | |
| Crust soaked to bottom | | | | | | | | | X | X | X | X | X | | | X | | X | | | | |
| **Meringue** | | | | | | | | | | | | | | | | | | | | | | |
| Watery or weeping | | | | | | | | | X | | | | | | | | | | X | X | X | |
| Tough | | | | | | | | | | X | | | | | | | | | X | X | X | X |

*Figure 5.2  Ordinary pie faults and their causes*

## A P P L E   P I E   F I L L I N G   ( c a n n e d )

| Apples, 1 No. 10 can | 6 lb | 8 oz |
|---|---|---|
| Water (1 qt) | 2 lb | |
| Sugar | 1 lb | 8 oz |
| Salt | | 1/2 oz |
| Cinnamon | | 1/4 oz |
| Nutmeg | | 1/8 oz |
| Butter | | 1 1/2 oz |
| Cornstarch | | 3 oz |
| | 10 lb | 5 3/8 oz |

*Method:* Bring to a boil all ingredients except cornstarch and 8 oz water. Dissolve cornstarch in water and add to mixture. Bring the mixture to a boil and remove from heat. For apple-raisin filling, add 8 ounces of raisins.

*Scaling instructions:* Five 9-inch pies.

*Baking instructions:* 425°F.

## A P P L E   P I E   F I L L I N G   ( f r o z e n )

| Apples (frozen) | 10 lb | |
|---|---|---|
| Water (1 1/4 qt) | 2 lb | 8 oz |
| Sugar | 1 lb | 8 oz |
| Salt | | 1/2 oz |
| Cinnamon | | 1/8 oz |
| Nutmeg | | 1/8 oz |
| Water (1/2 pint) | | 8 oz |
| Cornstarch | | 5 oz |
| Lemon juice (2 lemons) | | |
| Butter | | 3 oz |
| | 15 lb | 3/4 oz |

*Method:* Bring apples, water, sugar, and spices to a boil. Dissolve cornstarch in water and add. Cook to a boil and remove from heat. Add juice and butter and mix well.

*Scaling instructions:* Eight 9-inch pies.

*Baking instructions:* 425°F.

## BASIC CREAM FILLING
## or PASTRY CREAM FILLING

| | | |
|---|---|---|
| Milk (1 ¾ pints) | 1 lb | 12 oz |
| Sugar | | 3 oz |
| | | |
| Sugar | | 3 oz |
| Egg yolks | | 3 oz |
| Cake flour | | 1 ½ oz |
| Cornstarch | | 1 oz |
| Milk | | 4 oz |
| Butter | | ½ oz |
| Vanilla (to taste) | | |
| | 2 lb | 12 oz |

*Method:* Boil milk and sugar. Mix together sugar, yolks, flour, cornstarch, and milk, and add to hot milk and sugar, stirring continuously until mixture comes to a boil. Remove from heat. Stir butter and vanilla into mixture.

*Scaling instructions:* Two 9-inch pies.

*Chocolate filling:* Add 1 ½ oz of melted chocolate.

*Banana cream filling:* Slice into filling approximately 1 banana per pie.

*Coconut cream filling:* Add 2 oz of coconut per pie into mixture. Top with whipped cream.

## PASTRY CREAM (Crème Patissiere, Custard Cream)

Pastry cream plays an important part in the making of pastry. For this reason it must be well made. Smoothness and flavor are of special importance, and therefore great care must be taken during the mixing and boiling process.

Milk should be scalded with ½ of the sugar. The egg yolks must be well beaten with the rest of the sugar, flour, and cornstarch, until absolutely smooth. When milk is scalded, a part of the milk should be mixed with the egg mixture and then added to the first mixture and boiled together. It must be stirred continuously with a whip to prevent the cream from burning and at the same time to ensure a thorough mixing and a smooth cream.

Add the butter when cream is removed from the heat. This is also the time for adding the vanilla or other flavoring.

Never allow the sugar and eggs to stand without mixing because the sugar will curdle the eggs. Small hard lumps will form and you will have to strain your mixture before using it. In this way you will lose about ¼ of the value of the eggs, and the cream will be grainy instead of smooth. Therefore, it is very important that the sugar and eggs are mixed immediately.

Pastry cream should be cooled as fast as possible in a shallow pan (rather than a heavy pot) and refrigerated. Four precautions can be taken to prevent a heavy skin from forming on top of the cream:

1. Stir the cream occasionally as it cools to prevent a skin from forming.
2. After removing the cream from heat, place in a shallow pan to cool and top with small pats of butter. The butter will melt and form a protective coating.
3. Sprinkle top of the cream with granulated sugar while cooling. The sugar will melt and form a syrupy protective coating.
4. Place waxed paper or cellophane over the top of the cream. Cut some small holes in the paper for steam to escape while the cream cools.
5. Most important, always keep it refrigerated until use.

## Variations

Whipped cream may be folded into cold pastry cream for added richness.

Meringue may be folded into hot pastry cream for a fluffier, lighter cream.

A small amount of gelatin may be dissolved and mixed with either of the above variations to give the cream more body.

For other variations, chocolate, coffee, fruit, or any liqueur can be mixed into the cream.

## RAISIN PIE FILLING

| | | |
|---|---|---|
| Raisins | 3 lb | |
| Brown and granulated sugar | 1 lb | |
| Water (2 qt) | 4 lb | |
| Salt | | ¼ oz |
| Lemon (1 lemon) | | |
| Cinnamon | | ⅛ oz |
| Water (½ pint) | | 8 oz |
| Cornstarch | | 1 oz |
| Butter | | 1 oz |
| | 8 lb | 10⅜ oz |

*Method:* Boil together raisins, sugar, water, salt, lemon, and cinnamon. Dissolve cornstarch in 8 oz water and add to mixture. Bring to a boil and remove from heat. Add butter.

*Scaling instructions:* Four 9-inch pies.

*Baking instructions:* 425°F.

## CUSTARD PIE and COCONUT CUSTARD PIE FILLING

| | | |
|---|---|---|
| Milk (1 qt) | 2 lb | |
| Sugar | | 6 oz |
| Vanilla (to taste) | | |
| Nutmeg (to taste) | | |
| Eggs | | 10 oz |
| | 3 lb | |

*Method:* Beat all together.

*Scaling instructions:* Two 9-inch pies.

*Baking instructions:* Start at 450°F for 10 minutes and finish at 375°F.

*Coconut custard pie:* Butter coconut slightly, place in pie shell, pour mixture into shell, and bake.

## CHERRY PIE FILLING

| | | |
|---|---|---|
| Cherry juice (1 No. 10 can) | | |
| Sugar | 1 lb | |
| Salt | | 1/2 oz |
| Red color (2 drops) | | |
| Cornstarch | | 4 oz |
| Water | | 4 oz |
| Cherries, drained (1 No. 10 can) | | |
| Butter | | 1 oz |
| Sugar | 1 lb | 8 oz |
| Lemon juice (1 lemon) | | |
| | 3 lb | 1 1/2 oz |

*Method:* Bring cherry juice, sugar, salt, and coloring to a boil. Dissolve cornstarch in water and add to mixture. Bring to a boil and remove from heat. Add remaining ingredients.

*Scaling instructions:* Five 9-inch pies.

*Baking instructions:* 425°F.

## CHERRY PIE FILLING (frozen)

| | | |
|---|---|---|
| Cherry juice, drained from cherries | 3 lb | |
| Sugar | 1 lb | |
| Salt | | 1/4 oz |
| Red color (3 drops) | | |
| Water | | 8 oz |
| Cornstarch | | 5 oz |
| Sugar | 1 lb | |
| Cherries, drained | 7 lb | |
| Lemon juice (1 lemon) | | |
| | 12 lb | 13 1/4 oz |

*Method:* Bring cherry juice, sugar, salt, and coloring to a boil. Dissolve cornstarch in water and add. Bring to a boil and remove from heat. Add sugar, cherries, and lemon juice and mix in well.

*Scaling instructions:* Six 9-inch pies.

*Baking instructions:* 425°F.

## APRICOT PIE FILLING (frozen)

| | | |
|---|---|---|
| Apricots (frozen) | 10 lb | |
| Water (1 pint) | 1 lb | |
| Salt | | 1/4 oz |
| Sugar | 1 lb | |
| Yellow color (2 drops) | | |
| Water (1/2 pint) | | 8 oz |
| Cornstarch | | 5 oz |
| | 12 lb | 13 1/4 oz |

*Method:* Boil together apricots, water, salt, sugar, and coloring. Dissolve cornstarch in water and add to other ingredients. Cook to a boil and remove from heat.

*Scaling instructions:* Six 9-inch pies.
*Baking instructions:* 425°F.

## SWISS CHEESE PIE (Quiche filling)

| | | |
|---|---|---|
| Swiss cheese, grated | | 8 oz |
| Parmesan cheese, grated | | 8 oz |
| Egg yolks (4) | | |
| Salt and pepper (to taste) | | |
| Light cream (1 qt) | 2 lb | |
| Eggs (3) | | 6 oz |
| Onion, chopped fine (1 small) | | |
| Bacon, crisp, chopped fine | | 8 oz |
| Parsley, chopped fine | | |
| | 3 lb | 14 oz |

*Method:* Scald cream and mix cheeses, yolks, salt, pepper, and eggs into a custard. Sprinkle onion, bacon, and parsley on bottom of a prebaked pie shell. Pour custard mix over top.

*Baking instructions:* 350°–375°F for 10–15 minutes.

## PINEAPPLE CHIFFON PIE FILLING

| | | |
|---|---|---|
| Pineapple, crushed | 2 lb | |
| Sugar | 1 lb | |
| Water (1 qt) | 2 lb | |
| Salt | | 1/2 oz |
| Gelatin | | 1/4 oz |
| Yellow color (3 drops) | | |
| Cornstarch | | 5 oz |
| Water | | 5 oz |
| Egg whites | | 12 oz |
| Sugar | | 12 oz |
| | 7 lb | 2 3/4 oz |

*Method:* Bring pineapple, sugar, water, salt, gelatin, and coloring to a boil. Dissolve cornstarch in water and add to mixture. Bring to a boil and remove from heat. Beat whites and sugar into a meringue and fold into mixture. Top with whipped cream and toasted coconut.

*Scaling instructions:* Four 9-inch pies.

## PINEAPPLE PIE FILLING (No. 2)

| | | |
|---|---|---|
| Pineapple, crushed (1 No. 10 can) | 6 lb | 8 oz |
| Salt | | 1/4 oz |
| Corn syrup | | 8 oz |
| Sugar | 1 lb | 8 oz |
| Yellow color (3 drops) | | |
| Water (1 1/2 pints) | 1 lb | 8 oz |
| Cornstarch | | 3 oz |
| Water (1/2 pint) | | 8 oz |
| | 10 lb | 11 1/4 oz |

*Method:* Combine pineapple, salt, corn syrup, sugar, water, and coloring and bring to a boil. Dissolve cornstarch in water and add. Cook to a boil and remove from heat.

*Scaling instructions:* Five 9-inch pies.

*Baking instructions:* 425°F.

## BLUEBERRY PIE FILLING (frozen)

| | | |
|---|---|---|
| Blueberry, juice, drained from blueberries | 1 lb | |
| Water (1 pint) | 1 lb | |
| Sugar | 1 lb | 8 oz |
| Salt | | 1/4 oz |
| Water (1/2 pint) | | 8 oz |
| Cornstarch | | 4 oz |
| Sugar | 2 lb | |
| Blueberries, drained | 9 lb | |
| Lemon juice (2 lemons) | | |
| | 15 lb | 4 1/4 oz |

*Method:* Bring blueberry juice, water, sugar, and salt to a boil. Dissolve cornstarch in water and add. Cook to a boil and remove from heat. Add sugar, blueberries, and lemon juice and mix well.

*Scaling instructions:* Eight 9-inch pies.

*Baking instructions:* 425°F.

## PEACH PIE FILLING

| | | |
|---|---|---|
| Peach juice (1 No. 10 can) | | |
| Water (1 qt) | 2 lb | |
| Sugar | 1 lb | |
| Yellow color (3 drops) | | |
| Salt | | ¼ oz |
| Water (½ pint) | | 8 oz |
| Cornstarch | | 3 oz |
| Sugar | 1 lb | |
| Peaches (drained from No. 10 can) | 6 lb | 8 oz |
| | 11 lb | 3¼ oz |

*Method:* Bring juice, water, sugar, coloring, and salt to a boil. Dissolve cornstarch in water and add. Cook to a boil and remove from heat. Add sugar and peaches and mix well.

*Scaling instructions:* Five 9-inch pies.

*Baking instructions:* 425°F.

## LEMON PIE FILLING

| | | |
|---|---|---|
| Water (1 qt) | 2 lb | |
| Sugar | | 12 oz |
| Salt | | ½ oz |
| Butter | | 1 oz |
| Egg yolks | | 3 oz |
| Cornstarch | | 3 oz |
| Lemon juice | | 4 oz |
| | 3 lb | 7½ oz |

*Method:* Bring to a boil water, sugar, salt, and butter. Beat yolks, corn-starch, and lemon juice together and add. Bring to a boil and remove from heat.

*Scaling instructions:* Two 9-inch pies.

## LEMON CHIFFON PIE FILLING

| | | |
|---|---|---|
| Water (1 1/2 pints) | 1 lb | 8 oz |
| Sugar | 1 lb | |
| Salt | | 1/2 oz |
| Gelatin | | 3/4 oz |
| Egg yolks | | 8 oz |
| Lemon juice | | 8 oz |
| Cornstarch | | 4 oz |
| Water (1/2 pint) | | 8 oz |
| Egg whites | 1 lb | |
| Sugar | | 10 oz |
| | 5 lb | 15 1/4 oz |

*Method:* Bring water, sugar, salt, and gelatin to a boil. Dissolve yolks, juice, cornstarch, and water together and mix until smooth; add to mixture. Stir until the mixture comes to a boil and then remove from heat. Beat egg whites and sugar into a meringue and fold into hot mixture.

*Scaling instructions:* Four 9-inch pies.

*Orange chiffon pie:* Use 7 oz orange juice and 1 oz lemon juice.

## CHOCOLATE CHIFFON PIE

| | | |
|---|---|---|
| Water (1 qt) | 2 lb | |
| Gelatin | | 1/2 oz |
| Sugar | | 8 oz |
| Chocolate, bittersweet | | 4 oz |
| Salt | | 1/4 oz |
| Milk | | 6 oz |
| Cornstarch | | 4 oz |

| | | |
|---|---|---|
| Cream, heavy | | 6 oz |
| Vanilla (to taste) | | |
| Egg whites | | 12 oz |
| Sugar | | 8 oz |
| | 5 lb | 3/4 oz |

*Method:* Bring water, gelatin, sugar, chocolate, and salt to a boil. Dissolve cornstarch in milk, add to chocolate mixture, and bring to a boil. Remove from heat and add cream and vanilla. Beat whites and sugar into a meringue and fold into mixture. Place mixture into prebaked pie shells.

*Yield:* Four 9-inch pies.

## STRAWBERRY CHIFFON PIE FILLING

| | | |
|---|---|---|
| Strawberries, frozen | 2 lb | |
| Water (1 pint) | 1 lb | |
| Salt | | 1/4 oz |
| Sugar | | 8 oz |
| Red color (few drops) | | |
| Lemon juice (1 lemon) | | |
| Gelatin | | 1/4 oz |
| Cornstarch | | 4 oz |
| Water (1/2 pint) | | 8 oz |
| Egg whites | 1 lb | |
| Sugar | | 12 oz |
| | 6 lb | 1/2 oz |

*Method:* Bring strawberries, water, salt, sugar, coloring, juice, and gelatin to a boil. Dissolve cornstarch in water and add. Cook to a boil until thick and remove from heat. Beat whites and sugar into a meringue and fold into hot mixture.

*Scaling instructions:* Four 9-inch pies.

*Fresh fruit pie:* Use 2 lb of strawberries and 1 lb of sugar. Substitute raspberries for strawberries for raspberry chiffon pie.

## NESSELRODE PIE FILLING

| | | |
|---|---|---|
| Milk (1 qt) | 2 lb | |
| Gelatin | | 1 1/2 oz |
| Sugar | | 8 oz |
| Egg yolks (8 eggs) | | 6 oz |
| Heavy cream (1 qt) | 2 lb | |
| Sugar | | 4 oz |
| Nesselrode mixture* | | 10 oz |
| | 5 lb | 13 1/2 oz |

*Method:* Heat milk and gelatin to a boil. Mix sugar and yolks and add. Scald but *do not boil.* Remove from heat and cool. Whip cream and sugar until stiff and fold into mixture. Before doing so, be sure mixture is cool and starting to set. Fold in nesselrode mixture. Place in four prebaked shells. Top with whipped cream and shaved chocolate.

*Nesselrode mixture may be purchased or it may be prepared as follows: Soak together 2 oz each of cherries, pineapple, and raisins, 3 oz of chestnuts, and 1 oz of rum.

## SOUTHERN CHESS PIE

| | | |
|---|---|---|
| Brown sugar, light | 1 lb | |
| Cake flour | | 2 oz |
| Salt | | 1/2 oz |
| Milk solids | | 4 oz |
| Shortening and butter | | 8 oz |
| Brown sugar, light | 2 lb | |
| Eggs | | 12 oz |
| Vanilla (to taste) | | |
| Water, hot (1 qt) | 2 lb | |
| | 6 lb | 10 1/2 oz |

*Method:* Cream together sugar, flour, salt, milk solids, shortening, and butter. Beat in remaining sugar, eggs, vanilla, and cream. Add hot water in 3 stages.

*Baking instructions:* 400°F for 10 minutes; then 350°F until done.
*Yield:* 3 pies or 80 tarts.

*Pecan pie:* Add chopped pecans.

## SOUTHERN PECAN PIE FILLING

| | | |
|---|---|---|
| Pastry flour | | 2 oz |
| Granulated sugar | | 2 oz |
| Light Karo syrup (1 1/2 qt) | 3 lb | |
| Eggs, whole | 1 lb | |
| Vanilla (to taste) | | |
| Salt | | 1/2 oz |
| Butter, melted | | 3 oz |
| Pecans | | 8 oz |
| | 4 lb | 15 1/2 oz |

*Method:* Mix flour, sugar, and syrup together. Whip together eggs, vanilla, salt, and butter and add. Place 4 oz of pecans in each pie shell and pour mixture over this.
*Scaling instructions:* Two 9-inch pies.
*Baking instructions:* 325°F.

## PUMPKIN PIE FILLING

| | | |
|---|---|---|
| Brown and granulated sugar | 3 lb | |
| Bread flour | | 8 oz |
| Salt | | 1 oz |
| Cinnamon | | 1/2 oz |
| Cloves | | 1/4 oz |
| Ginger | | 1/8 oz |
| Pumpkin (1 No. 10 can) | 6 lb | 12 oz |
| Eggs | 1 lb | 4 oz |
| Skim milk (4 3/8 qt) | 8 lb | 12 oz |
| | 20 lb | 5 7/8 oz |

*Method:* Sift sugar, flour, and spices together. Add pumpkin, then eggs. Add milk.

*Scaling instructions:* Eight 9-inch pies.

*Baking instructions:* Let stand at least 3 to 4 hours before pouring into pie shell. Bake at 450°F for the first 10 minutes; then reduce heat to 375°F.

*Squash filling:* Substitute No. 10 can of squash for pumpkin.

*Sweet potato filling:* Substitute No. 10 can of sweet potatoes for pumpkin.

## M I N C E M E A T   P I E   F I L L I N G

| | | |
|---|---|---|
| Beef or venison | 6 lb | |
| Suet | 1 lb | |
| Apples, chopped | 4 lb | |
| Brown sugar | 1 lb | 8 oz |
| Raisins, seedless | 2 lb | 8 oz |
| Currants | 2 lb | 8 oz |
| Brandy (1/2 pint) | | 8 oz |
| Allspice | | 1/2 oz |
| Cloves | | 1/2 oz |
| | 18 lb | 1 oz |

*Method:* Boil meat and run through a grinder with suet. Add remaining ingredients and mix well. Add meat stock if more moisture is needed.

## D E L I G H T   F R U I T   E G G N O G   P I E

| | | |
|---|---|---|
| Unflavored gelatin | | 1 3/4 oz |
| Granulated sugar | 1 lb | 6 oz |
| Salt | | 1/2 oz |
| Egg yolks (16) | | 10 oz |
| Scalded milk (1 1/2 qt) | 3 lb | |
| Rum | | |
| Good brandy | | 8 oz |
| Egg whites (12) | | 12 oz |
| Whipped cream (1 1/2 pints) | 1 1/2 pts | |
| Fresh fruit | 1 lb | |
| | 8 lb | 14 1/4 oz |

*Method:* Stir gelatin, 1 lb of sugar, and salt together in a large round bowl. Place over a hot water bath (180°F), add milk and egg yolks, and continue whipping or stirring until all ingredients are well blended and mixture starts to thicken. Remove from heat, and place over ice or cool in the refrigerator. Stir occasionally to expedite the cooling. When mixture starts to set, add rum and brandy. Mix thoroughly. Beat egg whites to soft peaks; gradually add the remaining sugar. In the meantime, fold whipped cream into the yolk mixture, and then immediately fold in the egg whites. Pour into prebaked and pre- pared pie shells. Cool in the refrigerator, garnish with whipped cream and cut glazed fresh fruit. Yield: 4 10-inch pies.

*Preparing pie shells for fruit eggnog pie:* Use prebaked pie shells. When cool, sprinkle the bottom with sliced fresh strawberries, whole blueberries, or fine-sliced peaches or pineapple. Pour filling over fruit. This delicious pie can be served accompanied with a sauce of your choice.

## KEY LIME PIE

This famous lime pie recipe originated in the South Florida Keys.

| | | |
|---|---|---|
| Egg yolks (36) | 1 lb | 8 oz |
| Sweetened condensed milk | 4 lb | 8 oz |
| Lime rinds (3), grated | | |
| Lime juice (3 cups) | 1 lb | 8 oz |
| Egg whites (16) | 1 lb | |
| Sugar | 2 lb | |
| | 10 lb | 8 oz |

*Method:* Blend egg yolks, condensed milk, and lime rinds together. Add lime juice. Pour into prebaked pie shells.

*Baking instructions:* 375°F oven on baking sheets for 10 minutes or until set. Remove from oven, and cool thoroughly. Beat egg whites stiff, adding sugar gradually. Cover the pie evenly with the meringue. Dust with XXXX sugar and place in 400°F oven.

# CHAPTER SIX

# PUDDINGS

# AND SAUCES

Puddings are popular, economical, and profitable desserts. As with other products, careful preparation is necessary to obtain the best results. All too often, puddings are carelessly prepared. The result is a mediocre product.

There are five basic types of puddings. The three most popular in commercial food operations are boiled puddings, baked puddings, and chilled puddings.

Steamed puddings are usually served during the cold season. They are generally heavy and are served with a hot sauce. They may be very attractive if care is taken with the final preparation.

Soufflé puddings are adaptable to à la carte service. They must be made just before serving to secure lightness and fluffiness; otherwise, they will become heavy and soggy. Soufflés are not a wise choice for cafeteria service.

## BASIC VANILLA PUDDING

| | | |
|---|---|---|
| Milk (1 qt) | 2 lb | |
| Sugar | | 4 oz |
| Egg yolks | | 2 oz |
| Sugar | | 4 oz |
| Cornstarch | | 1 1/2 oz |

Vanilla (to taste)

| Butter | | ¹/₂ oz |
|---|---|---|
| | 2 lb | 12 oz |

*Method:* Mix sugar and milk, and scald. Mix together yolks, sugar, and cornstarch, and add part of the milk. Add rest of milk and boil, then remove from heat. Add vanilla and butter and mix well.

*Yield:* 10 servings.

*Variations:* Chocolate or other flavoring.

## BREAD AND BUTTER PUDDING

| Milk (1 qt) | 2 lb | |
|---|---|---|
| Sugar | | 4 oz |
| Salt (to taste) | | |
| Vanilla (to taste) | | |
| Nutmeg (to taste) | | |
| Eggs | | 2 oz |
| Bread slices (10 slices) | | |
| | 2 lb | 6 oz |

*Method:* Scald milk. Beat together sugar, salt, vanilla, nutmeg, and eggs, and add to milk. Remove crust from bread, slice thin, brush with butter, and cut each slice in half. Place bread slices in a pudding dish, overlapping each slice. Sprinkle with a few raisins and pour custard mixture over slices. Serve hot with cream.

*Baking instructions:* Place dish on a pan containing water and bake at 400°F until firm.

## BASIC BLANCMANGE

| Milk (1 qt) | 2 lb | |
|---|---|---|
| Sugar | | 8 oz |
| Gelatin | | ³/₄ oz |
| Cream, whipped | 1 lb | |
| | 3 lb | 8³/₄ oz |

*Method:* Scald milk, sugar, and gelatin. Put aside to cool and set. Fold in whipped cream and pour into individual molds (rinsed with cold water). Chill. Serve with crushed fruit or cream.

*Chocolate blancmange:* Add 4 ounces of chocolate.

*Coconut blancmange:* Add 8 ounces of toasted coconut.

*Nut blancmange:* Add 8 ounces of nut meats.

## OLD ENGLISH PLUM PUDDING

| | | |
|---|---|---|
| Suet (ground) | 2 lb | |
| Sultanas | 1 lb | |
| Currants | 1 lb | |
| Brown sugar | | 12 oz |
| Lemon peel | | 4 oz |
| Orange peel | | 4 oz |
| Citron | | 4 oz |
| Salt | | 1 oz |
| Nutmeg | | 1/4 oz |
| Allspice | | 1/4 oz |
| Ginger | | 1/4 oz |
| Lemon juice (2 lemons) | | |
| Rum (1 pint) | | |
| Eggs | | 8 oz |
| Bread flour | 1 lb | |
| Bread crumbs | 1 lb | |
| | 8 lb | 1 3/4 oz |

*Method:* Boil together for 2 hours suet, sultanas, currants, sugar, peels, citron, spices, and lemon juice. Store in a well-covered container for about 1 week. Add rum. Add eggs and mix. Add flour and bread crumbs and mix. Fill containers about 7/8 full. Steam for about 2 hours. Serve with a brandy sauce or hard sauce.

## PLUM PUDDING

| | | |
|---|---|---|
| Butter | 1 lb | |
| Brown sugar | 1 lb | |
| Salt | | 1 oz |
| Nutmeg | | 1/4 oz |
| Allspice | | 1/4 oz |
| Ginger | | 1/4 oz |
| Eggs | 1 lb | |
| Molasses | 1 lb | |
| Rum (1/2 pint) | | 8 oz |
| Brandy (1/2 pint) | | 8 oz |
| Bread flour | 1 lb | |
| Raisins and sultanas | 3 lb | |
| Currants | 3 lb | |
| Citron | 1 lb | |
| Orange peel | 1 lb | |
| Lemon peel | | 8 oz |
| Bread crumbs | 1 lb | |
| | 15 lb | 9 3/4 oz |

*Method:* Cream together butter, sugar, salt, and spices. Add eggs and mix thoroughly. Beat in molasses, rum, and brandy. Mix in flour and fruit and stir until smooth. Add bread crumbs and mix to proper consistency. Fill containers approximately 7/8 full and steam for about 2 hours. Serve with brandy sauce or hard sauce.

## TAPIOCA

| | | |
|---|---|---|
| Milk (1 qt) | 2 lb | |
| Minute tapioca | | 2 1/2 oz |
| Salt (to taste) | | |
| Egg yolks | | 2 oz |
| Sugar | | 2 1/2 oz |
| Egg whites (3) | | |
| Sugar | | 2 1/2 oz |
| Vanilla (to taste) | | |
| | 2 lb | 9 1/2 oz |

*Method:* Boil milk and cook tapioca until transparent. Remove from heat and add yolks and sugar. Whip together. Whip sugar, whites, and vanilla into a meringue and fold into mixture.

*Yield:* 10 servings.

## CABINET PUDDING

| | | |
|---|---|---|
| Milk (1 qt) | 2 lb | |
| Sugar | | 6 oz |
| Eggs | | 10 oz |
| Vanilla (to taste) | | |
| Sponge cake, plain | | 8 oz |
| Raisins | | 4 oz |
| | 3 lb | 12 oz |

*Method:* Combine milk, sugar, eggs, and vanilla and cook into a custard. Butter 12 custard cups and dredge with sugar. Cut sponge cake into 1/2-inch cubes. Place cake cubes in the cups and sprinkle with raisins. Pour the custard over this. Place the cups in a pan with water and bake until custard is firm. Turn out on a serving dish and serve with a hot vanilla sauce.

*Baking instructions:* 400°F.

*Diplomat pudding:* Substitute diced candied fruit for the raisins. Proceed as above.

## BROWNIE PUDDING

| | | |
|---|---|---|
| Cake flour | 1 lb | |
| Baking powder | | 1 oz |
| Salt | | 1/4 oz |
| Sugar | 1 lb | 4 oz |
| Cocoa | | 2 oz |
| Shortening, melted | | 4 oz |
| Milk (1 pint) | 1 lb | |
| Vanilla (to taste) | | |
| Walnuts | | 8 oz |

| | | |
|---|---|---|
| Brown sugar | 1 lb | 8 oz |
| Cocoa | | 4 oz |
| Water, hot (1 1/2 qt) | 3 lb | |
| | 6 lb | 4 oz |

*Method:* Sift dry ingredients together and work in shortening. Mix in milk, add walnuts and vanilla, and place this mixture in a 12 × 18-inch pudding pan. Pour hot water on top of mixture in pudding pan.

*Baking instructions:* 375°F.

## INDIAN PUDDING

| | | |
|---|---|---|
| Milk (1 1/2 qt) | 3 lb | |
| Yellow cornmeal | | 8 oz |
| Molasses | | 8 oz |
| Sugar | | 4 oz |
| Salt | | 1/4 oz |
| Ginger | | 1/2 oz |
| | 4 lb | 4 3/4 oz |

*Method:* Cook milk and cornmeal in a double boiler about 20 minutes and remove from heat. Add remaining ingredients and place in a deep pudding pan. Serve with ice cream.

*Baking instructions:* Two hours at 375°F in water bath, stirring pudding occasionally.

*Yield:* 10 servings.

## COCONUT PUDDING

| | | |
|---|---|---|
| Granulated sugar | 1 lb | 8 oz |
| Butter | | 12 oz |
| Salt | | 1/2 oz |
| Egg whites | 1 lb | 8 oz |
| Shredded coconut | 1 lb | |
| Cake flour | 1 lb | 8 oz |
| Baking powder | | 3/4 oz |
| | 6 lb | 5 1/4 oz |

*Method:* Lightly cream sugar, butter, and salt. Add egg whites and cream. Add remaining ingredients and mix until smooth. Fill steam-type pudding pans ³/₄ full and place cover on top. Steam for 1¹/₂ hours. Serve with hot vanilla custard sauce.

*Baking instructions:* 375°F.

# CUP CUSTARDS

| | | |
|---|---|---|
| Milk (1 qt) | 2 lb | |
| Sugar | | 8 oz |
| Eggs (6) | | 10 oz |
| Vanilla (to taste) | | |
| | 3 lb | 2 oz |

*Method:* Mix together sugar, eggs, and vanilla, and add to milk. Place in 10 custard cups. Place in pan with water and bake until firm.

*Baking instructions:* 400°F.

*Caramel custard:* Boil together 2 lb of granulated sugar and 1 lb of water to 328°F or until it becomes a dark amber color. Pour ¹/₄ inch of this syrup into dry custard cups. Place above custard mixture into same cups and treat as with cup custards. When baked and cold, turn custard out into a deep dish and serve.

# BASIC VANILLA BAVARIAN PUDDING

| | | |
|---|---|---|
| Milk (1 qt) | 2 lb | |
| Gelatin | | 1¹/₂ oz |
| Sugar | | 4 oz |
| Vanilla (to taste) | | |
| Heavy cream | | 8 oz |
| Egg whites | | 8 oz |
| Sugar | | 4 oz |
| | 3 lb | 9¹/₂ oz |

*Method:* Dissolve gelatin in part of milk and bring rest of milk and sugar to a boil. Remove from heat and add dissolved gelatin. Add vanilla after mixture cools. Whip cream and fold in. Whip whites and sugar into a meringue and fold in. Place in custard cups or pudding dishes and put into refrigerator to set. When set, unmold into cold serving dishes and serve with a sauce.

*Variations:* Chocolate, walnut, coffee, and strawberry.

## BASIC VANILLA SOUFFLÉ

| | |
|---|---|
| Bread flour | 3 oz |
| Butter | 3 oz |
| Milk | 8 oz |
| Egg yolks | 6 oz |
| Egg whites | 8 oz |
| Sugar | 6 oz |
| Vanilla (to taste) | |
| Salt (to taste) | |
| 2 lb | 2 oz |

*Method:* Put together flour and butter into a paste. Bring milk to a boil and add to flour paste. Cook. Beat in egg yolks as for a cream puff mixture. Whip egg whites, sugar, salt, and vanilla into a soft-peak meringue and fold into above. Butter soufflé cups or soufflé dish and dredge with granulated sugar. Fill to top with mixture and bake until done. Serve with a vanilla custard sauce.

*Baking instructions:* 400°F with water on bottom of pan.

*Chocolate soufflé:* Add melted chocolate with egg yolks and proceed as for vanilla. Serve with vanilla sauce.

*Cheese soufflé:* Add grated cheese with egg yolks and omit sugar from meringue. Dredge soufflé cups or dish with grated cheese instead of sugar.

# BAVARIAN CREAM

| | | |
|---|---|---|
| Milk (1 qt) | 2 lb | |
| Egg yolks (6) | | 4 oz |
| Sugar | | 8 oz |
| Gelatin, plain | | 1/2 oz |
| Heavy cream (1 pint) | 1 lb | |
| | 3 lb | 12 1/2 oz |

*Method:* Heat milk. Beat together yolks, sugar, and gelatin, and add to milk, but *do not boil.* Whip cream and fold into mixture after it has cooled and started to thicken. Place into a mold or cup and allow to set until firm. Unmold and serve with a sauce.

*Variations:* Coffee, chocolate, walnut, or maple.

# BLUEBERRY PUDDING

| | | |
|---|---|---|
| Sugar | 1 lb | 8 oz |
| Butter | | 12 oz |
| Salt | | 1/2 oz |
| Egg whites | 1 lb | |
| Milk | | 12 oz |
| Cake flour | 1 lb | 8 oz |
| Baking powder | | 3/4 oz |
| Cinnamon (to taste) | | |
| Blueberries, fresh | 1 lb | 8 oz |
| | 7 lb | 1 1/4 oz |

*Method:* Cream sugar, butter, and salt together lightly. Add whites and cream. Add milk. Sift together flour, baking powder, and cinnamon, add, and mix until smooth. Fold blueberries into this mixture. Fill steam-type pudding pans 3/4 full and place cover on top. Steam for 1 1/2 hours and serve with hard sauce or lemon sauce.

## WINE CREAM (Bavarian)

| | | |
|---|---|---|
| Wine (medium dry, not too sweet) | 1 lb | 14 oz |
| Sugar | | 8 oz |
| Egg yolks (16) | | 10 oz |
| Juice of 1 lemon | | |
| Sugar | | 2 oz |
| Wine | | 2 oz |
| Gelatin | | 1 oz |
| Liquid (wine, water, etc.) | | 8 oz |
| Heavy cream | 2 lb | |
| | 5 lb | 13 oz |

*Method:* Heat first wine and first sugar together. Prepare liaison from egg yolks, lemon juice, and second wine and sugar; temper and add to the wine base as for making crème anglaise. Cook to nappe, remove from heat immediately, and strain through chinois. Prepare gelatine by sprinkling it over liquid; let sit for 5 minutes. Place in double boiler and melt to a temperature of 110°F. Pour gelatin solution into first mixture and cool by stirring over ice. Whip heavy cream (slightly underwhipped, with or without added sugar). When first mixture reaches 60–65°F, add the whipped cream in two steps. (Be careful not to overmix so much that aeration is lost, yet be sure to incorporate to prevent streaky mixture.) Fill molds immediately after the mix is completed and refrigerate.

## CRÈME CARAMEL

| | | |
|---|---|---|
| *Step 1* | | |
| Sugar | | 8 oz |
| Fresh lemon juice | | 1 oz |
| Water | | 2 oz |
| *Step 2* | | |
| Milk | 2 lb | |
| Eggs (8) | | 13 oz |
| Yolks (4) | | 3 oz |
| Sugar | | 8 oz |
| Vanilla (to taste) | | |
| | 4 lb | 3 oz |

*Method:* Butter the sides of 14 4-oz cups. Carmelize the first sugar to a rich caramel and carefully divide between bottoms of cups. Bring milk to a boil and remove from heat (if using vanilla bean, steep in the hot milk). Temper together the eggs and hot milk. *Do not return to heat.* Add vanilla flavoring. Divide the custard mixture between the cups.

*Baking instructions:* Place the cups in a bain marie and bake at 350°F for 35 minutes or until custard has set. Refrigerate overnight before turning out and serving. Yields 14 4-oz portions.

*Note:* The dissolved caramel that appears when the custards are turned out is actually the sauce for this dessert.

## RICE CUSTARD PUDDING

| | | |
|---|---|---|
| Milk (1 qt) | 2 lb | |
| Rice | | 4 oz |
| Salt (to taste) | | |
| Sugar | | 4 oz |
| Egg yolks (2) | | 1½ oz |
| Vanilla (to taste) | | |
| Heavy cream | | 5 oz |
| | 2 lb | 14½ oz |

*Method:* Boil milk, add rice and salt, and simmer until rice is tender. Mix together sugar, yolks, and vanilla, and add. Cook until thick, remove from heat, and cool. Add cream after it sets.

*Yield:* 10 servings.

## FARINA PUDDING

| | | |
|---|---|---|
| Milk (2 qt) | 4 lb | |
| Farina | | 6 oz |
| Egg yolks (4) | | 4 oz |
| Sugar | | 6 oz |
| Cream | | 8 oz |
| | 5 lb | 8 oz |

*Method:* Boil milk in a double boiler. Add farina and cook to a mush. Remove from heat. Beat together remaining ingredients and add. Pour into pudding pans or dishes and bake in a water bath. Serve hot with cream.

*Yield:* 15 portions.

*Baking instructions:* 400°F.

## SAUCES FOR PUDDINGS AND ICE CREAMS

There are three basic sauces from which a great many varieties may be made by the addition of various ingredients.

*Cream sauce* is the most popular. It is made from milk, sugar, eggs or egg yolks, and water, cooked to a very soft custard, flavored, and served either hot or cold.

*Fruit sauce* is made from fruit or fruit juice boiled with water and flavored. Lemon juice is then added and the whole is reduced or thickened with a small amount of starch. Then it is cooked until it becomes a thin, jellylike sauce.

*Hard sauce* consists of powdered sugar and butter, creamed lightly, and sometimes thinned down with cream or egg and flavored. Hard sauce is always served cold on hot puddings or dumplings.

# CRÈME BRÛLÉE

| | | |
|---|---|---|
| Egg yolks (10) | | 7 oz |
| Eggs (4) | | 6 oz |
| Brown sugar | | 8 oz |
| Light cream (1 qt) | 2 lb | |
| Vanilla bean | | |
| | 3 lb | 5 oz |

*Method:* Beat yolks, eggs, and sugar until creamy and fluffy. Heat the cream with the vanilla bean to boiling point. Remove from heat, and stir gradually into the egg mixture. Blend well and place over a hot water bath until mixture starts to thicken and coats the spoon. Remove from heat and cool on ice, stirring from time to time to speed the cooling. Remove vanilla bean, and pour cold custard into deep individual earthenware serving cups.

Sprinkle the top heavily with brown sugar. Brown carefully under a hot broiler until the sugar caramelizes. Serve cold. Yield: 10–12 servings.

## FLOATING ISLAND

| | | |
|---|---|---|
| Milk (1 ½ qt) | 3 lb | |
| Egg whites (6) | | 6 oz |
| Sugar | | 5 oz |
| Egg yolks (10) | | 7 oz |
| Vanilla flavoring (1 teaspoon) | | ⅙ oz |
| | 4 lb | 2⅙ oz |

*Method:* Bring milk to a boil in a deep saucepan. Beat egg whites stiff, gradually adding 3 oz sugar and vanilla. With a large spoon, scoop out a portion of the egg white (approximately the size of an egg), add to the milk, and poach for 1–2 minutes or until firm. Continue until all the egg white has been used. Milk should be simmering during this process. Lift the meringue from the hot milk, and place on a towel to dry. Beat the yolks with remaining sugar. Remove milk from heat, and add to the yolk mixture, stirring well to blend all ingredients. Return to the fire, and cook mixture carefully until the sauce coats the spoon. Do not boil. Strain. When mixture starts to thicken, remove from heat, cool on ice, and pour into individual dishes or one large serving bowl. Using a fork dipped in hot caramel sugar, stripe each meringue. Place meringue into the sauce so it floats on top. Yield: 8–10 servings.

## CHOCOLATE SAUCE

| | |
|---|---|
| Sugar | 3 lb |
| Water (1 ½ qt) | 3 lb |
| Corn syrup | 1 lb |
| Bittersweet chocolate, chopped fine | 2 lb |
| Sweet chocolate, chopped fine | 2 lb |
| Heavy cream (1 qt) | 2 lb |
| | 13 lb |

*Method:* Combine all ingredients except cream. Bring to a boil and stir. Boil heavy cream and stir in.

## BUTTERSCOTCH SAUCE

| | | |
|---|---|---|
| Brown sugar | 2 lb | |
| Water | 1 lb | |
| Corn syrup | | 8 oz |
| Butter | | 8 oz |
| Heavy cream | 2 lb | |
| | 6 lb | |

*Method:* Combine sugar, corn syrup, and water; bring to a boil until temperature reaches 320°F. Add butter. Add cream and place on fire for a few minutes. Use for ice cream sundaes.

## LEMON CUSTARD SAUCE

| | | |
|---|---|---|
| Water (2 qt) | 4 lb | |
| Sugar | | 8 oz |
| Egg yolks | | 8 oz |
| Cornstarch | | 1 oz |
| Coloring (few drops) | | |
| Sugar | | 8 oz |
| Lemon juice | | 8 oz |
| Lemon rind (4 lemons) | | |
| | 6 lb | 1 oz |

*Method:* Bring water and sugar to a boil. Beat together yolks, cornstarch, coloring, and sugar. Add to water and thicken. Boil for 1 minute and remove from heat. Add lemon juice and rind and mix.

*Orange sauce:* Substitute oranges for lemons.

## VANILLA CUSTARD SAUCE

| | | |
|---|---|---|
| Light cream (1 qt) | 2 lb | |
| Egg yolks | | 6 oz |
| Sugar | | 8 oz |
| Vanilla (to taste) | | |
| | 2 lb | 14 oz |

*Method:* Bring cream to a boil. Mix yolks, sugar, and vanilla together and add. Cook until thick, but do not allow to come to a boil.

## APRICOT SAUCE

| | | |
|---|---|---|
| Apricots (1 No. 10 can) | 6 lb | 12 oz |
| Water (2 qt) | 4 lb | |
| Sugar | 4 lb | |
| Lemon juice (2 lemons) | | |
| Cornstarch | | 2 oz |
| Water (1 pint) | 1 lb | |
| | 15 lb | 14 oz |

*Method:* Press apricots and water through a fine sieve. Add sugar and lemon juice and bring to a boil. Dissolve cornstarch in water and add. Allow to boil 1 minute and remove from heat. Strain and cool. Sauce may be served hot or cold.

*Peach sauce:* Substitute peaches for apricots.

## RASPBERRY SAUCE

| | | |
|---|---|---|
| Raspberries, fresh (2 qt) | 1 lb | 8 oz |
| Sugar | 2 lb | |
| Lemon juice (2 lemons) | | |
| Water (1 pint) | 1 lb | |
| Coloring (few drops) | | |

ary to purchase a uniform fondant icing from a bakers' supply
his is done, the prepared fondant should be stored in contain-
th a damp cloth or with a small amount of water, to prevent
ut.

t icing is to be used, the desired quantity should be taken
over a warm bath to 98° to 100°F, stirring constantly. This
nd causes it to flow freely. If it is still too heavy, a simple
ed to thin it more. Flavoring or coloring may be added as
icing should not be heated above 100°F or it will lose its
ate a dull finish.

primarily for pouring and dipping. It may be used as a
gs such as butter cream by creaming the butter or short-
dant. This creates fluffier icings.

r cream is made by creaming together sugar, butter or short-
e last are added to give the icing the desired consistency.
ming depends upon the lightness required in the finished
n may be colored and flavored as desired. When not in use,
tored in a cool place with wax paper covering.
nerally used for layer cakes and decorated cakes.

e icing, the sugar is cooked into a syrup in order to
required. When this hot syrup is added to the balance
he formula, it creates a rather heavy body. Before the
cake it should be heated slightly in a water bath. When
be stored and covered to prevent spoilage and drying.
ally used on cupcakes and layer cakes.

r Icing. This is a simple icing, whose basic ingredi-
, corn syrup, and flavoring—are mixed well together.
g to coffee cake, Danish pastry, and the like, heat it
and or pastry brush. Flat icing is usually white and
lemon. Coloring may be used, but very sparingly, if
vered when not in use.

s made by cooking a syrup of sugar, water, and
dded to beaten egg whites while hot. A heavy or
he heaviness or thinness of the syrup. Boiled icing
illa and colored lightly. It should be applied gen-
n the cake. It breaks down if stored overnight and
e desired amounts as needed.

| | | |
|---|---|---|
| Cornstarch | | 2 oz |
| Water | | 8 oz |
| | 5 lb | 2 oz |

*Method:* Boil together raspberries, sugar, juice, water and coloring. Dissolve cornstarch in water and add. Boil for about 1 minute. Remove from heat and strain.

*Strawberry sauce:* Substitute strawberries for raspberries.

## MELBA SAUCE

| | | |
|---|---|---|
| Raspberries, fresh | 1 lb | |
| Currant jelly | | 8 oz |
| Sugar | | 8 oz |
| Water | | 2 oz |
| Cornstarch | | 1 oz |
| | 2 lb | 3 oz |

*Method:* Boil raspberries, jelly, and sugar together. Dissolve cornstarch in water and add. Bring to a boil.

## HARD SAUCE

| | | |
|---|---|---|
| Powdered sugar | | 2 lb |
| Butter | | 1 lb |
| | | 3 lb |

*Method:* Cream lightly. Eggs or cream may be used to bring to the desired consistency.

*Variations:* Mocha, chocolate, or brandy may be added.

## WILD TURKEY CRÈME ANGLAISE

| | | |
|---|---|---|
| Egg yolks (8) | | 5 oz |
| Sugar | | 7 oz |
| Wild Turkey liquor | | 1 oz |
| Whipped cream | 1 lb | |
| | 1 lb | 13 oz |

*Method:* Beat yolks and sugar over double boiler until thick. Cool. Add liquor. Fold in whipped cream.

C H A P T E R

# I C I

Attractive icings have three
around the cake, improving
they improve the taste; and
more attractive item for sal

Proper combinations of
should be used. There is
destroy the taste and qual
for fruit icings when it is

Care should be taken
in dark icings, which
eye appeal, but too m
should be studied care
little color than to ad

## BASIC ICINGS

There are seven
marshmallow, and

*Fondant.* Fonda
perature of 240
quickly until it
Fondant is

become custo
house. When
ers, covered w
it from drying

When fonda
out and heated
thins the icing
syrup may be u
desired. Fondant
glossiness and cr

Fondant is use
base for other ici
ening with the for

*Butter Cream.* Butte
ening, and eggs. Th
The amount of crea
product. Butter crea
this icing should be
Butter cream is g

*Fudge Icing.* For fud
obtain the smoothnes
of the ingredients in
icing is applied to the
it is not in use it shoul
Fudge icing is gene

*Flat Icing or Plain Wa*
ents—water, icing suga
Before applying this ici
to 100°F and apply by
flavored with vanilla or
at all. It must be kept co

*Boiled Icing.* This icing
glucose, which is then a
thin icing depends upon t
may be flavored with var
erously and left in peaks
should be made only in th

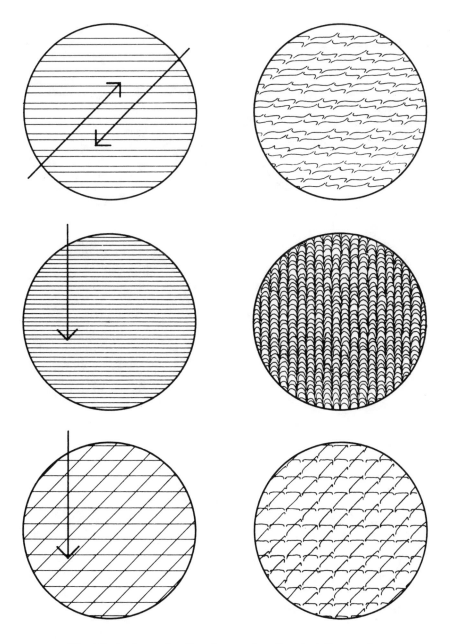

After icing has been put on the cake, a gentle action of a knife drawn in the directions indicated will give pleasing effects.

Figure 7.1   Cake decorating

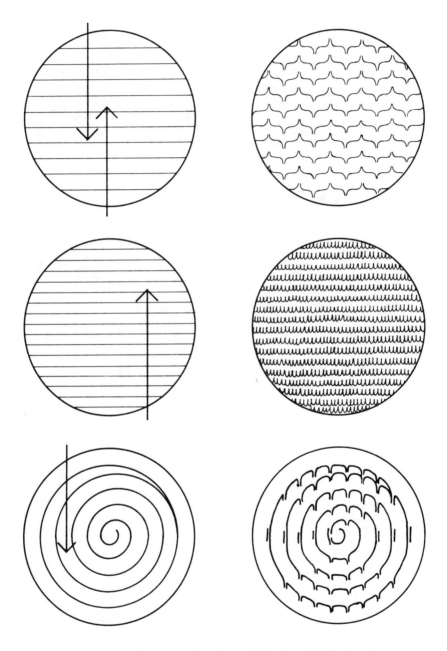

After icing has been put on the cake, a gentle action of a knife drawn in
the directions indicated will give pleasing effects.

*Figure 7.2   Cake decorating*

*Marshmallow Icing.* Marshmallow icing is a variation of boiled icing, but it has a stabilizer—usually gelatin and confectioner's sugar—added to it. It is applied in the same manner as boiled icing.

*Royal or Decorating Icing.* Royal or decorating icing is also a fairly simple icing to make. Icing sugar, egg whites, and an acid agent are beaten together into a smooth consistency. Royal icing is used primarily for decorating and for flower making. It is also often used to make cake "dummies," but seldom used on stable cakes as it tends to become hard and brittle. It may be colored as desired and should be covered with a damp cloth when not in use.

## FLAT ICING

| Confectioners' sugar | 5 lb | |
|---|---|---|
| Corn syrup | | 8 oz |
| Egg whites | | 4 oz |
| Water, hot | | 12 oz (variable) |
| | 6 lb | 8 oz |

*Method:* Mix ingredients until smooth. Heat icing as needed and apply only to precooled products. Use it for coffee cake, Danish pastry, etc.

## PLAIN ICING

| Confectioners' sugar | 5 lb | |
|---|---|---|
| Water | | 8 oz |
| Egg whites | | 1 oz |
| Corn syrup | | 4 oz |
| | 5 lb | 13 oz |

*Method:* Mix ingredients together until smooth. This icing is an excellent substitute for fondant icing. It must be heated to 98°F and flavored the same as for fondant.

## MARSHMALLOW ICING

| | | |
|---|---|---|
| Water, cold (1 qt) | 2 lb | |
| Gelatin (plain granular) | | 3 oz |
| Corn syrup | 1 lb | |
| Confectioners' sugar | 6 lb | 8 oz |
| Salt | | 1/2 oz |
| Vanilla (to taste) | | |
| Egg whites | | 8 oz |
| | 10 lb | 3 1/2 oz |

*Method:* Soak gelatin in water, and heat until dissolved. Add sugar, syrup, salt, and vanilla, and mix. Add whites and beat to a proper consistency. Use this icing directly after mixing. For a more tender icing, add 3 ounces of shortening for each pound of icing.

## ROYAL OR DECORATING ICING

| | | |
|---|---|---|
| Confectioners' sugar | 2 lb | |
| Egg whites | | 6 oz (variable) |
| Cream of tartar (1/4 teaspoon) | | |
| | 2 lb | 6 oz |

*Method:* Beat together until stiff. Use for decorating dummies, making flowers, lattice work, etc. Keep covered with a damp towel when not in use.

## FONDANT ICING

| | |
|---|---|
| Granulated sugar | 10 lb |
| Water (1 qt) | 2 lb |
| Corn syrup | 1 lb |
| | 13 lb |

*Method:* Boil ingredients to approximately 240°F. Pour hot syrup on wet marble slab. Sprinkle water over hot syrup to prevent it from crystallizing.

Allow it to cool to about 110°F. Work with a spatula from the sides to the center until the syrup becomes stiff and white in color. Remove from marble. Place in a storage container and cover tightly with a damp cloth. Use as needed.

## WHITE FUDGE ICING

| | | |
|---|---|---|
| Milk (1 pint) | 1 lb (variable) | |
| Shortening, emulsified | | 8 oz |
| Butter | | 8 oz |
| Salt | | ¼ oz |
| Confectioners' sugar | 7 lb | |
| Vanilla (to taste) | | |
| | 9 lb | ¼ oz |

*Method:* Heat milk, shortening, butter, and salt to 160°F. Add sugar and vanilla and mix until smooth. Icing will be easier to apply while it is still warm.

## BOILED ICING

| | | |
|---|---|---|
| Egg whites | 2 lb | |
| Salt | | 1 oz |
| Granulated sugar | 4 lb | |
| Glucose | | 8 oz |
| Water (1 pint) | 1 lb | |
| | 7 lb | 9 oz |

*Method:* Beat whites and salt slowly to a wet peak. Boil sugar, glucose, and water to 240°F and add slowly to egg whites. Beat to the proper consistency. Make only enough for immediate use.

## BUTTER CREAM ICING

| | | |
|---|---|---|
| Confectioners' sugar | 10 lb | |
| Shortening, emulsified | 2 lb | 8 oz |
| Butter | 2 lb | 8 oz |
| Salt | | 1/2 oz |
| Flavoring (to taste) | | |
| Egg whites | 1 lb | |
| Lemon juice | | 1 oz |
| | 16 lb | 1 1/2 oz |

*Method:* Cream together lightly sugar, shortening, butter, salt, and flavoring. Add egg whites and lemon juice and cream to desired lightness.

## FRENCH BUTTER CREAM ICING

| | | |
|---|---|---|
| Eggs (4 whole) | | 8 oz |
| Egg yolks (8) | | 6 oz |
| Sugar | 4 lb | |
| Water (1 pint) | 1 lb | |
| Butter | 3 lb | |
| Shortening, Hi-ratio | 1 lb | |
| Vanilla (to taste) | | |
| | 9 lb | 14 oz |

*Method:* Whip eggs and yolks until light. Cook sugar and water to 238°F and beat into eggs until cool. Add butter and shortening and whip. Add vanilla.

## MAKING AND USING THE PAPER CONE

Practically any design or pattern may be made with a paper cone. Cut wax, or preferably parchment, paper into a triangle-shaped piece. Then roll the paper into shape. Fill the cone with the desired icing, roll the top down, and snip off the bottom to the desired shape or size. Royal icing is by far the most economical to use for practice work.

The use of a paper cone requires practice. Too often the student starts practicing on a design that is too complicated. One should start with a series of straight lines until the right pressure and pull of the icing is acquired. Practice and practice only will give the right dexterity and perfection desired.

Many designs may be copied with the aid of a paper cone, such as birds, flowers, and latticework. Those who can master this type of work can be of extra value to themselves and the trade.

## FRENCH BUTTER CREAM

| | | |
|---|---|---|
| Egg yolks (11) | | 8 oz |
| Whole eggs (8) | | 12 oz |
| Sugar | 6 lb | |
| Water (1½ pints) | 1 lb | 8 oz |
| Butter (at room temperature) | 6 lb | |
| | 14 lb | 12 oz |

*Method:* Combine yolks, eggs, sugar, and water, and warm in a double boiler to 110°F. Mix until light and fluffy. Cream butter until lightened and beat into egg mixture until well incorporated. Flavor as desired.

## ITALIAN BUTTER CREAM

| | | |
|---|---|---|
| Sugar | 5 lb | |
| Water (1½ pints) | 1 lb | 8 oz |
| Egg whites (80) | 5 lb | |
| Butter | 10 lb | |
| | 21 lb | 8 oz |

*Method:* Combine sugar and water in a heavy pan and cook to 240°F. Place egg whites in a mixing bowl and beat to medium-stiff peaks. In a slow, steady stream, add boiling sugar to whipped whites. Continue to whip until mixture has cooled to room temperature. Whip in butter by adding in small quantities. Flavor as desired.

## GERMAN BUTTER CREAM

| | | |
|---|---|---|
| Butter | 1 lb | |
| Pastry cream | 2 lb | |
| | 3 lb | |

*Method:* Cream the butter in a mixing bowl. Gradually add the pastry cream and cream together.

## DEVIL FUDGE ICING

| | | |
|---|---|---|
| Cocoa | 1 lb | |
| Shortening and butter | 1 lb | |
| Corn syrup | 1 lb | 8 oz |
| Salt | | 1 oz |
| Vanilla (to taste) | | |
| Water, hot (1 pint) | 1 lb (variable) | |
| Confectioners' sugar | 5 lb | |
| | 9 lb | 9 oz |

*Method:* Cream together until smooth cocoa, butter and shortening, syrup, salt, and vanilla. Add hot water and mix well. Add sugar and mix until smooth.

## CHOCOLATE FUDGE ICING

| | | |
|---|---|---|
| Granulated sugar | 3 lb | |
| Water (1 pint) | 1 lb | |
| Salt | | 1/4 oz |
| Corn syrup | 1 lb | |
| Bitter chocolate | 1 lb | |
| Confectioners' sugar | 1 lb | 8 oz |
| Butter | | 4 oz |
| Vanilla (to taste) | | |
| | 7 lb | 12 1/4 oz |

1. Cut square diagonally.

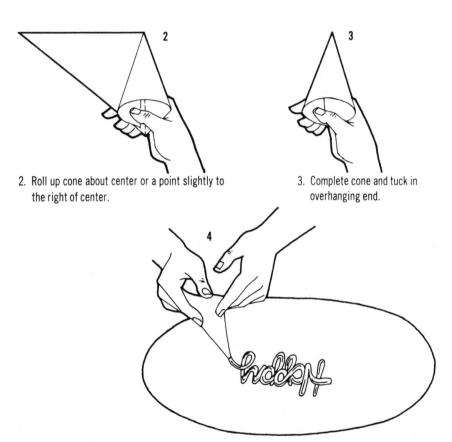

2. Roll up cone about center or a point slightly to the right of center.

3. Complete cone and tuck in overhanging end.

4. Fill with icing and apply with pressure of thumb, using other hand to steady the cone.

*Figure 7.3   Decorating cones*

*Figure 7.4  Decorating birthday cakes*

*Method:* Boil sugar, water, salt, and corn syrup to 238°F and remove from heat. Add chocolate and stir until it is melted. Cream together sugar, butter, and vanilla. Pour into mixture while still hot and mix at slow speed until the proper consistency is obtained. Icing is easier to apply while still warm.

## DECORATING BIRTHDAY CAKES

Prepare a cake circle 2 inches larger than the cake and a doily 2 inches larger than the cake circle. Put a little icing between the cake circle and doily. Make sure cake is level and free of crumbs. Place a little icing between the doily and the cake before icing. This will hold the cake in place.

*Icing.* Place cake in center of circle and doily. Start icing the side of the cake to ¼-inch thickness. After the side is done, place icing in the center of the cake and spread to cover the complete cake.

*Decorating.* First, place writing on cake. Second, put on the border. Put on the flowers and other decorations last.

## PIPING JELLY CAKE TRANSFERS

Piping jelly is used to transfer pictures onto the top of a cake as a decoration. In the accompanying example, a Viking ship is used. First a suitable picture is chosen and a sheet of tracing paper is placed over it. The figure is then traced with black or brown piping jelly outline. The outline is then filled in with appropriate colors of piping jelly. This design is then allowed to dry overnight.

The cake is then prepared and iced to receive the jelly transfer. The transfer is placed on the cake, jelly side to the icing, with the paper side up. It is recommended that the surface of the paper be wetted, either with a brush or cotton dipped in water, and allowed to stand a minute or so to facilitate release of the paper from the jelly. Peel the paper off, and you have the complete transfer of the original picture to the top of a cake.

Good sources for cake illustrations are children's coloring books and magazines. Piping jelly is available in neutral or in various colors.

*Figure 7.5   Piping jelly cake transfers*

*Figure 7.6   Piping jelly cake transfers*

*Figure 7.7   Piping jelly cake transfers*

# CHAPTER EIGHT

# ASSORTED PASTRIES

# AND DESSERTS

The modern pastry chef and baker realize that they must have many variations in their desserts in order to attract new patrons. Although fancy pastries are usually referred to as "French pastries," many nations have contributed hundreds of popular variations to these popular desserts.

Some pastries and desserts are known in the trade as standard types. They may be greatly improved by developing variations and creating special names for them in the hotels and restaurants where they are prepared.

The finest-quality ingredients obtainable must be used for these pastries. Patient craftsmanship is necessary for a fine finished product.

Originality and ingenuity, plus careful selection for variety of pastries and desserts have created famous reputations for many hotels and restaurants.

## PUFF PASTE AND PUFF PASTE VARIATIONS

Puff Paste is a rolled pastry from which a wide variety of flaky and fine-tasting products are made.

No other baked product is quite like puff paste. It contains no sugar or leavening agent, yet it rises to eight times its original size. This is due to the process of rolling alternate layers of fat and dough. (There are often well over 1000 layers.) A product that is only 1/4 inch high before baking sometimes rises to over 2 inches with hundreds of fine flakes. A finished puff paste is tender and crisp.

Some bakers feel that the addition of cream of tartar helps the dough to rise. However, properly made puff paste rises without the addition of cream of tartar to help it.

## Rules for Preparing Puff Paste

Great care must be taken in preparing and rolling puff paste, or the finished product will not be up to standard. The following rules should be observed:

1. Scale and prepare dough strictly according to formula.
2. When butter or puff paste shortening is rolled into the dough, it must be the same consistency as the dough. Poor dough will result if one is stiffer than the other.
3. In warm climates or bakeshops, dough should be kept under refrigeration after it is rolled.
4. Care must be taken to make sure every particle of the puff paste shortening or butter is evenly distributed through the dough. All end corners should be folded squarely.
5. All excess flour should be brushed off before folding dough.
6. A minimum of 20 to 30 minutes should be allowed before folding the dough.
7. If paste is left over from the preceding day, it will require additional rolling before being cut. Otherwise dough will not develop properly during baking.
8. After dough is cut, it should stand for 20 to 30 minutes before baking. This prevents excessive shrinkage.
9. Puff paste should be baked until it is dry and crisp.

*Figure 8.1   Roll the dough following the direction of the four corners; leave the center somewhat thicker*

| Method | Ingredients | lb | oz | Cost per lb | Cost |
|---|---|---|---|---|---|
| 1. Make into a dough. Remove from mixer. Round into a ball shape. Allow to stand 15 to 20 minutes. | Bread flour | 5 | | | |
| | Salt | | 1 | | |
| | Butter | | 8 | | |
| | Eggs (5 eggs) | | 8 | | |
| | Cold water | 2 | 4 | | |
| 2. Roll Step 1 into Step 2. Directions for this process are given below. | Butter or Puff Paste Shortening | 5 | | | |
| **Total Yield**: about 100 | | | | | |
| **Scaling Instructions** | | | | Cost per oz | |
| **Baking Temperature:** | | | | Cost per lb | |
| 350°–375°F. for 20–25 minutes | | | | | |

*Figure 8.2 Name of product: puff paste dough*

## Rolling in and Folding Puff Paste

1. Roll the dough following the direction of the four corners (Figure 8.1). Leave the center somewhat thicker.
2. Place shortening in center (Figure 8.3) and lap over the four sides (Figure 8.4). Flatten with a rolling pin by gently pounding dough (Figure 8.5).
3. Roll out again about 1/2 inch thick and twice as long as it is wide.
4. After brushing off all excess flour, fold both ends toward middle and then double again (Figure 8.6).

*Figure 8.3  Place shortening in center
and lap over the four sides; flatten with
a rolling pin by gently pounding dough*

*Figure 8.4  Roll out again about ¹/₂ inch
thick and twice as long as it is wide*

5. Allow the dough to stand in a cool place or put in the refrigerator for
   at least 20 to 30 minutes.
6. Repeat the rolling process four times. On the final roll, make a "three-
   way fold" (Figure 8.7).

**Cream Slices**

1. Roll out a piece of puff paste ¹/₈ inch thick. Brush entire surface with
   water. Sprinkle with sliced almonds or filberts.
2. Using a pastry wheel, cut dough into 2 × 4-inch oblongs.
3. Place on sheet pans and allow to stand 30 minutes. Bake in 375°F
   oven for 20–25 minutes.
4. After baking, split in two. Fill with whipped cream. Dust with confectioners' sugar.

*Figure 8.5   After brushing off all excess flour, fold both ends toward middle and then double again*

*Figure 8.6   Allow the dough to stand in a cool place or put in the refrigerator for at least 20–30 minutes*

### Cheese Sticks

1. Give two turns to a 1-lb piece of puff paste. Dust between folds with 2 oz grated cheese mixed with salt and paprika.
2. Roll out to about ¹⁄₆ inch thick into strips 1 inch wide.
3. Roll these strips into twisted sticks. Place on wet sheet pans. Allow to stand 30 minutes.
4. Bake in 375°F oven for 20–25 minutes. After baking, cut into strips 4 inches in length. Serve.

### Napoleons

1. Roll 1¹⁄₂ lb puff paste scraps very thin. Roll to the size of a baking pan.
2. Place on pan and allow to stand for 30 minutes. Prick all over to prevent blistering while baking.

*Figure 8.7 Repeat the rolling process four times; on the final roll, make a "three way fold"*

3. Bake in 375°F oven for 20–25 minutes.
4. After baking, cut into three strips. Place one on top of the other with vanilla-flavored pastry cream between layers.
5. Frost the top with one or more flavors of fondant icing.
6. When fondant is dry, cut into bars about 4 × 2 inches long.

**Patty Shells**

1. Roll out a piece of puff paste dough to about ⅛ inch thick.
2. Using a 3-inch scalloped-edge cutter, cut out rounds. Place rounds on a clean, wet baking pan.
3. Roll out another piece of puff paste dough to ¼-inch thick. Be sure thickness is uniform.
4. Using the same cutter as before, cut into rounds. Then, using a 2-inch scalloped-edge cutter, cut a hole in the center of each round.
5. Wash the first rounds with water. Then carefully place the rings cut from the second rounds on top of the washed rounds.
6. Wash with an egg wash. Allow to stand for at least 30 minutes.
7. Bake in a 375°F oven for 20–25 minutes.
Note: Greased paper placed over the top of the patty shells before they are baked prevents them from toppling over.

**Turnovers**

1. Roll out puff paste dough ⅛ inch thick. Cut into 5-inch squares.
2. Wash surface of squares with water; fold cornerwise to form triangle. (Filling may be put into these turnovers before folding, or they may be baked without filling.)

*Figure 8.8 Rolling and folding puff paste*

3. Allow to stand about 30 minutes.
4. Bake in 375°F oven for 20–25 minutes.
5. If baked without filling, turnovers may be split with a knife and filled with a variety of fruit fillings.

## Vol-au-Vent

1. Follow directions for patty shells given at left. Vol-au-vent is merely a large patty shell, somewhat thicker in proportion to its diameter.

*Figure 8.9    1*, Napoleons; *2*, vol-au-vent patty shell; *3*, cream slices; *4*, cream horns or lady locks; *5*, turnovers; *6*, cheese sticks

2. A top crust for the shell can be made from the center cut from the second round.
3. Top crust is more attractive if it is scored before baking. Pattern for scoring is shown above.

### Cream Horns (Lady Locks)

1. Roll puff paste into a strip about 15 inches wide and 48 inches long. When the rolling is completed, pastry should be no more than ⅛ inch thick.
2. Cut into strips about ¼ inch wide. Wash surface with water. Roll each strip on a cream horn tin, starting the strip on the small end of the tin and following a diagonal direction. When the tin is covered, roll the horns in granulated sugar. Place in baking pans.
3. Allow to rest before baking to reduce shrinkage.
4. Bake in a 375°F oven until lightly browned. Remove tins from the baked horns. Fill with marshmallow filling or whipped cream.

### Palm Leaves (Pigs' Ears)

1. Sprinkle work bench with granulated sugar. Roll out a 1-lb piece of puff paste dough to ⅛ inch thick; sprinkle top with sugar.
2. Fold dough toward the center from both ends; repeat a second time. (See diagram above.)
3. Cut in ¼-inch slices. Place on solid sheet pan; allow to stand 15–20 minutes.
4. Bake in 400°F oven. Turn over when half done to color both sides. (This also aids in caramelizing the sugar.)

*Figure 8.10 Depositing cream puff shells*

*Figure 8.11 Depositing éclair shells*

*Figure 8.12 Shaping basket handles and swans' necks from éclair paste*

*Figure 8.13 Making croutons with éclair paste*

## Butterflies

1. Roll out scraps of puff paste dough. Layer 2 or 3 flat pieces of dough one on top of the other.
2. Brush a narrow strip down the center of each layer with water. Make an impression with rolling pin.
3. Cut into $1/2$-inch pieces perpendicular to the impression. Give piece a half twist (with cut side up). Lay a small ($1/4$ × 2-inch) piece across the center of twisted piece to form body.
4. Allow to stand 15–20 minutes. Bake in 400°F oven. Turn over when half done to color both sides.

## Apple Strudel—Made in Puff Paste

1. Roll out puff paste paper thin into a 6 × 24-inch sheet. Place on a paper-lined solid sheet pan.
2. Add sponge cake crumbs to apple filling mixture, using enough to absorb excess liquid.
3. Place apple mixture in center of dough. Brush edges with egg wash.
4. Roll out a cover (the same size as bottom). Fold in half lengthwise. Cut to $2/3$ the width.
5. Cover apple mixture with second piece of dough; trim excess and seal well with fingers.
6. Brush surface with egg wash.
7. Allow to stand 20 minutes. Bake in 375°F over for 20–25 minutes.
Note: For variation, cherries, blueberries, or your favorite fruit filling may be used.

## Pinwheels

1. Roll out a piece of puff paste dough to ¹/₈ inch thick. Cut into ¹/₄-inch squares.
2. Make four incisions in each square. Use a sharp knife. These incisions are made at each corner and reach to within 1 inch of the center (see diagram).
3. Brush the center of each square with egg wash. Fold each corner to the center (see second diagram); press firmly. This forms the pinwheel from which this pastry gets its name.
4. Brush the surfaces with egg wash. Place a dab of fruit preserves in the center of each pinwheel.
5. Place on pans. Allow to stand for a few minutes. Bake in a 350°F oven for 20–25 minutes.

## Pâte Dome

1. Roll out puff paste dough to ¹/₄ inch thick. Cut out one 8-inch circle for base and one 10-inch circle for top.
2. Wash entire surface of the bottom round with water.
3. Roll and ball up parchment paper into round dome shape. Cover with aluminum foil. Place in center of washed bottom round. (See illustration.)
4. Cover with the 10-inch round of dough.
5. Seal bottom securely. Notch entire outer bottom edge with paring knife.
6. Roll out scraps of puff paste dough. Cut a ¹/₄-inch circular band for around the bottom. Cut another ¹/₄-inch circular band and place about 2 inches from top. (This piece acts as cutting guide for the finished product.)
7. Cut four ¹/₄-inch strips and place on dome to divide it into quarters. Cut out desired designs and place within the quarters. (see illustration.) Wash entire surface. Allow to stand 30 minutes. Bake in 375°F oven for 20–25 minutes.

Note: *After* pâte has baked about 10 minutes, one or two small cuts can be made to allow moisture to escape.

## Four Fingers

1. Roll out a rectangle of puff paste dough using sugar to roll out instead of flour.
2. Mark the center lengthwise and fold the sides to the center. Next mark the center crosswise and fold along this line (see diagram). Fold once again along the original center and press together.

3. Slice and bake as for palm leaves.
4. Fingers may be sandwiched in pairs with butter cream.

**Pithivier**

1. Roll out puff paste to ¼ inch thick. Cut out two 8-inch rounds. Wash entire surface of one round with water.
2. Place a mound of franchipan in the center of this round. Cover with second round and secure bottom.
3. Roll out scraps of puff paste dough to ¼ inch thick. Cut out a ¼-inch circular band 8 inches in diameter. Place this ring around the bottom of the franchipan-filled rounds. Cut small slits all around bottom.
4. Brush surface with egg wash.
5. Cut a swirl design all around the mound with small paring knife.
6. Allow to stand for 30 minutes; bake in 375°F oven for 20–25 minutes. (If pithivier becomes too brown, it may be covered with greased brown paper.)
7. Remove from oven when baked. Sprinkle liberally with powdered sugar and return to oven for glazing.

## PUFF PASTE DOUGH

| | | |
|---|---|---|
| Bread flour | 5 lb | |
| Salt | | 1 oz |
| Butter | | 8 oz |
| Eggs | | 8 oz |
| Water, cold (1 ⅛ qt) | 2 lb | 4 oz |
| Butter for puff paste | 5 lb | |
| | 13 lb | 5 oz |

*Method:* Make flour, salt, butter, eggs, and water into a dough. Remove from mixer, round into a ball, and allow to stand for 15 to 20 minutes. Roll butter into dough. Directions for this process follow.

*Baking instructions:* 350°–375°F.

*Variations:* Patty shells, vol-au-vent, cream horns, cheese sticks, cream slices, turnovers, napoleons, butterfly, etc.

## TECHNIQUES FOR PREPARING ÉCLAIR AND CREAM PUFF PASTE DESSERTS

| Method | Ingredients | lb | oz | Cost per lb | Cost |
|---|---|---|---|---|---|
| 1. Bring to a good rolling boil. | Water or milk | 2 | | | |
| | Shortening or butter | 1 | | | |
| | Salt | | ½ | | |
| 2. Combine with Step 1; blend. Cook until the mixture is smooth and rolls free from side of pot. Remove from heat. | Bread flour | 1 | 8 | | |
| 3. Add slowly until a medium-stiff paste is obtained. Blend well after each addition of eggs. | Eggs (variable— about 24) | 2 | 8 | | |
| **Total** | | | | | |
| **Scaling Instructions** | | **Cost per Oz.** | | | |
| **Baking Temperature:** 400°F for a good half hour | | **Cost per Lb.** | | | |

**Remarks**: Paper may be used on pans, or they may be lightly greased.

*Figure 8.14 Name of product: éclair and cream puff paste (pâte à chou)*

## Precautions

1. Make sure that the shortening and water are brought to a good rolling boil.
2. Improper cooking of Step 1. (Be sure shortening is melted.)
3. Mixture in Step 2 should be dry when cooked and not stick to pot.
4. Consistency of mix is very important. Common mistakes are using too many eggs and using too few eggs.
5. Incorrect addition of eggs must be avoided. (Add only 2 or 3 at a time, blending in well after each addition.)
6. Shell must not be removed from oven until it is completely dry or it will collapse.

*Figure 8.15   Croquembouche*

## Croquembouche

To make a croquembouche, first make approximately 60 1-inch cream puffs, or as many as required for the size you wish. Cool; fill with pastry cream. Next dip one puff at a time into hot caramel syrup and set inside a circle of nougat or pastry. Place a second circle of puffs on top of the first layer. Continue to build a pyramid of six to nine layers of puffs, decreasing the size of each circle.

For an interesting effect, use nougat candy to make upper and lower ornament as pictured, using your own design if desired.

**To make the nougat,** combine 1 lb granulated sugar with the juice of 1/4 lemon; cook in a sauce pan until the syrup is a golden brown. Remove from heat and add 12 oz warm sliced almonds. (Sesame seeds may be substituted for sliced almonds.) Spread the mixture onto an oiled marble slab, roll out

*Figure 8.16   Polka tart*

with a lightly oiled rolling pin, and cut with a lightly oiled knife (or cutters) to desired shapes. To keep nougat from becoming cool while working, place in a warm oven (250°F). After cutting into desired shapes, allow to cool and harden.

To hold pieces of nougat together, use carmelized sugar. Dip the pieces to be affixed and hold in position until set. Continue this until all pieces are assembled.

Finish by decorating edges with small dots of royal icing. Set crown on croquembouche before serving.

For the crown effect used in Figure 8.8, small triangular shapes were cut and cooled over a lightly oiled rolling pin. A 4-inch circle and a 2-inch circle were then cut out, and the pieces were then affixed by the method described.

**Polka Tart**

1. Roll out pie crust or pastry dough about ⅛ inch thick. Cut a circle about 8 inches in diameter for a large tart, 3 inches in diameter for an individual tart.
2. Place dough on a baking sheet lined with baking paper. Using a plain tube, dress out a rim of cream puff paste around the edge.
3. Bake at 400°F for 30 minutes or until golden brown. Cool; fill with pastry cream.
4. Place a generous amount of granulated sugar on top of pastry cream. Caramelize the sugar by pressing a red hot poker on top of the pastry.

**French Doughnuts**

1. Heat fat in a kettle to 375°F.
2. Cut a piece of heavy paper to ½ the size of the kettle.

*Figure 8.17   French doughnuts*

*Figure 8.18   Cream puff swan*

3. Fill pastry bag with cream puff paste. Using a star tube, dress out rings
   2½ to 3 inches in diameter on the heavy paper. Keep rings well apart.
4. Take paper in both hands and insert it into the kettle of hot fat (paper
   side up). The rings will drop off into the fat.
5. Allow doughnuts to fry for 10 minutes or until golden brown on one
   side. Then flip over and allow the other side to brown. Remove from
   fat and drain well.
6. French doughnuts may be split and filled with jam or pastry cream or
   iced with a plain flat icing.

## Cream Puff Swan

1. Using a pastry bag and tube with a ¼-inch opening, form the head

*Figure 8.19   Éclairs*

and neck of the swan from cream puff paste. Paste should be dressed
out to form a question mark.

2. Using a cream puff shell, cut off the top third. Then cut this into two
   pieces to be used as wings.
3. Fill the remainder of the cream puff shell with whipped cream or pastry
   cream. Place wing, neck, and head in position in the filling. Dust with
   confectioners' sugar.

## Éclairs

1. Line a baking sheet with paper or grease it lightly.
2. Fill a pastry bag with cream puff paste. Using a plain ½-inch tube,
   dress out fingers 3 to 4 inches in length. Space well apart.
3. Bake at 400°F for 30 minutes or until dry. Cool.
4. Fill with pastry cream, whipped cream, or a combination of both. (Ice
   cream may also be used.) Ice with flavored fondant or top with sauce.

*Figure 8.20   Cream puff shells*

## Cream Puff Shells, Baskets

1. Using a plain ½-inch tube and pastry bag, dress out cream puff paste onto paper-lined or lightly greased baking pans. Puffs should be about 2 inches in diameter when dressed out. Space well apart to permit uniform baking.
2. Bake at 400°F for 30 minutes or until dry and golden brown. Cool.
3. Fill with pastry cream, whipped cream, a combination of both, or ice cream. Frost with your favorite icing or top with sauce.
4. Cream puff baskets are made by removing the top of the cream puff shell, filling and inserting handle as shown in the illustration. (Handles should be dressed out using a pastry tube with a ¼-inch opening. Make them in the shape of a ring.)
5. Cream puff fantasies are made in the same manner as cream puff baskets, except that three smaller circles are inserted into the filling rather than the one large circle that acts as the handle of the basket.

## Banana Surprise

1. Make a curved éclair shell. Split shell in two. Each shell makes two desserts.
2. Fill shell with pastry cream or ice cream.
3. Cut a banana into four quarters and place on top of filling.
4. Top with chocolate sauce and sprinkle with toasted sliced almonds.

## St. Honoré

1. Dress out 15 1-inch cream puff shells and bake.

*Figure 8.21   Cream puff baskets*

*Figure 8.22   Banana surprise*

2. Roll out pie crust or pastry dough to about ⅛ inch thick. Cut a circle 8 inches in diameter. Place dough on a sheet pan lined with paper.
3. With a plain tube, dress out a rim of cream puff paste around the edge of the pastry. (Use the same technique as for polka tart.)
4. Bake in a 400°F oven for 30 minutes or until dry and golden brown. Cool.
5. Dip the small cream puff shells (Step No. 1) into carmelized sugar and

*Figure 8.23   St. Honoré*

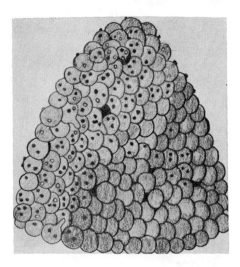

*Figure 8.24   Honeybee Hive*

place on the rim of the larger baked circle. Affix with additional car-melized sugar.

6. Fill the center of the pastry with a bavarian cream or pastry cream.
7. Garnish with cherries and serve.

## Honeybee Hive

1. Line a baking sheet with paper. Using a ½-inch plain tube and pastry bag, dress out ¼-inch balls of cream puff paste onto pan.
2. Bake in 400°F oven for 15–18 minutes until dry. Cool.

*Figure 8.25 Beignet soufflé*

*Figure 8.26 Profiteroles (hors d'oeuvre puffs)*

3. Dip these small puffs into a mixture of 4 parts honey and 1 part granulated sugar boiled together.
4. Arrange puffs on a platter, stacking them in the shape of a bee hive.
5. Sprinkle with nonpareils.

Note: Also used to garnish soups.

**Beignet Soufflé**

1. Heat fat to 370°F. Dress cream puff paste onto paper.
2. Place balls in deep fat using the same technique as for French doughnuts. (If preferred, cream puff paste can be dropped by the spoonful directly into the hot fat.)
3. Fry in hot fat until golden brown on all sides. Serve with saboyon sauce or dust with confectioner's sugar.

**Profiteroles (Hors d'Oeuvre Puffs)**

1. Using a plain tube, dress out 1-inch balls of cream puff paste.
2. Bake in 400°F oven for about 20 minutes or until dry. Cool.

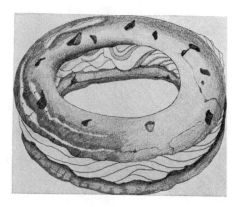

*Figure 8.27   Turban*

3. Split shells and fill with whipped cream, pastry cream, bavarian cream, or any comparable mixture.
4. Frost with flavored fondant icing. Garnish with nuts, fruits, etc.

**Note:** The famous **profiteroles au chocolat** are filled with ice cream and served with a thin chocolate sauce.

The puffs may also be filled with savory mixtures and served as cocktail hors d'oeuvres.

### Turban

1. Trace a 6- to 8-inch circle on a paper-lined baking sheet.
2. Using a plain pastry tube, dress out a circular band of cream puff paste about 1½ inch thick.
3. Brush with egg wash. Sprinkle with raw sliced almonds.
4. Bake in 400°F oven for about 30 minutes or until dry. Cool.
5. Split the ring horizontally. Fill with whipped cream or pastry cream. Place top back on ring and dust with confectioners' sugar.

## CREAM PUFF AND ÉCLAIR PASTE

| Water or milk (1 qt) | 2 lb | |
|---|---|---|
| Shortening or butter | 1 lb | |
| Bread flour | 1 lb | 8 oz |
| Eggs* | 2 lb | 8 oz |
| | 7 lb | |

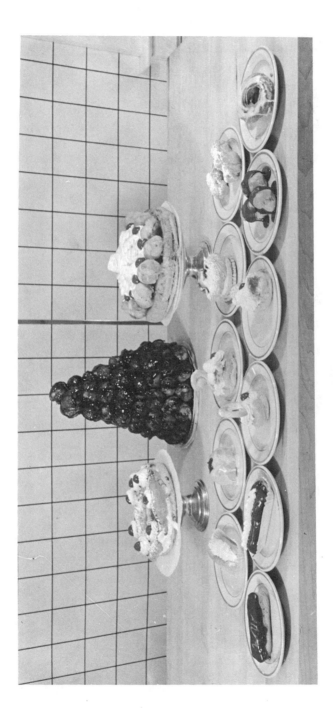

*Figure 8.28*  Top: *Turban, croquembouche, and gateau Saint Honoré;* center: *whipped cream éclair, cream puff, swan cream puff, polka tart, and beignet soufflé;* front row: *chocolate éclair, chocolate whipped cream éclair, basket cream éclair, butterfly cream puff, profiterole au chocolat, and French cruller*

*Method:* Bring liquid and shortening to a rolling boil. Combine with flour and cook until the mixture is smooth and rolls free from the sides of the pot. Add eggs slowly until a medium-stiff paste is obtained.

*Baking instructions:* 400°F.

*Variations:* Cream puffs, éclairs, French crullers, and profiteroles.

*The number of eggs varies. It is important that this mixture be of the right consistency or the product will be below par. Too few eggs will give a small product; too many will cause the product to spread.

## SAINT HONORÉ

Saint Honoré consists of four parts: (1) short paste such as pie crust, (2) éclair paste or pâte à chou, (3) miniature puffs or small balls of éclair paste, and (4) pastry cream filling.

Roll out pie crust to an 8-inch diameter and ⅛ inch thick. Put small holes in crust to prevent blistering. Egg wash the edge of the crust. Pipe éclair paste on top of the edges of the pie crust, using a pastry bag with a plain round tube. Bake in oven at 400°F until done. When crust is cold, cut a ½-inch slice from the top of the shell. Fill edge with cream filling and put the top back on. Fill eight miniature puffs with cream filling from the bottom.

Cook ⅓ weight water to ⅔ weight of sugar at 325°F to make caramel sugar. Dip bottom of puffs in caramel sugar and arrange on the edge of the pie with the sticky side down.

For the center filling, use a basic cream filling and fold whipped egg whites into it. Fill center of shell with this mixture and garnish with a red cherry in the center and cherry halves between each miniature puff. Dust puffs with powdered sugar. Chill in refrigerator before serving. Serves 8.

## APPLE STRUDEL

| | |
|---|---|
| Bread flour, all-purpose | 5 oz |
| Pastry flour, all-purpose | 3 oz |
| Salt | 1/8 oz |
| Egg (1 whole) | 2 oz |
| Shortening | 1/4 oz |
| Water | 4 oz |
| | 14 3/8 oz |

*Method:* Mix ingredients into a smooth dough. Shape into a ball and brush with vegetable oil. Let dough relax for 30 minutes. Spread dough on a 36 × 36-inch cloth and stretch thin and transparent (like tissue paper). This dough will make a 30-inch square. Brush entire surface with butter; egg wash bottom.

## FILLING

| | | |
|---|---|---|
| Apples, chopped | 2 lb | |
| Bread crumbs | | 4 oz |
| Brown sugar | | 2 oz |
| Granulated sugar | | 2 oz |
| Raisins | | 2 oz |
| Walnuts or almonds | | 2 oz |
| Cinnamon | | 1/8 oz |
| Lemon juice (1/2 lemon) | | |
| Salt (to taste) | | |
| | 2 lb | 12 1/8 oz |

*Method:* Spread filling, leaving 2 inches on each side and fold ends under. Roll like a jelly roll, cut in half, and place on paper-lined pan. Brush with butter. Bake at 400°F for 45 minutes. Serve with whipped cream.

*Figure 8.29   Folding apple dumplings*

## APPLE DUMPLINGS

Roll out pie dough approximately ⅛ inch thick and cut into 6-inch squares. Brush the squares with water.

Place apples that are about 3 inches in diameter, peeled and cored, on each square. Fill the center of the apples with a mixture of cinnamon sugar, fold as shown in Figure 8.29, and bake at 400°F. Serve hot with lemon sauce or hard sauce.

## RAISED DOUGHNUTS

| | | |
|---|---|---|
| Salt | | 1 oz |
| Sugar | | 6 oz |
| Shortening | | 6 oz |
| Flavoring (to taste) | | |
| Eggs | | 8 oz |
| Water (1 qt) | 2 lb | |
| Yeast | | 3 oz |
| Milk solids | | 4 oz |
| Bread flour | 3 lb | 8 oz |
| | 7 lb | 4 oz |

*Method:* Mix into a straight dough. Ferment for 1 hour and 30 minutes. Always check: frying temperature frequently during frying, dough temperature, condition of fat, and condition of equipment.

*Scaling instructions:* 1 lb per dozen.

*Frying instructions:* Fry at 375°F.

| Problem / Cause | Machine speed too fast | Dough too hot | Dough too cold | Doughnuts turned too soon after rising to fat surface | Old shortening | Insufficient cutter overlap | Overmixing of dough | Cutter size too small | Undermixing of dough | New shortening | Dough too old | Excessive cutter overlap | Frying temp. too high | Frying temp. too low | Cutter in poor condition | Dough too stiff | Dough too soft | Frying time excessive |
|---|---|---|---|---|---|---|---|---|---|---|---|---|---|---|---|---|---|---|
| Toughness | | | | | | X | | | X | | | X | | | | X | | |
| Excessive fat absorption | X | X | | X | | X | | | X | | X | X | X | | | X | X | |
| Lack of expansion | X | | | | | X | | | | X | X | X | | X | X | X | X | |
| Excessive expansion | X | | | | | | X | | | | | | | | | | X | |
| Excessive core | X | X | X | | | X | X | | | | | X | X | | | X | | |
| Knotty doughnuts | X | X | | X | | X | | | | | X | X | | | X | X | | |
| Fat absorption too low | X | | X | | | X | | | X | | | X | | | X | | | |
| Poor break (in frying) | X | X | | | X | X | | | | | | X | | X | X | | | |
| "Balling up" of doughnuts | X | X | | X | X | | X | | | | | X | | | | | | |
| Tight, ringy doughnuts | X | X | | X | | X | | | X | | X | X | | X | X | X | | |
| Cracking on bottom | | X | | | | X | | X | X | | | | X | | | X | | |
| Cracking inside ring | X | X | | X | | | | X | | X | | | X | | X | | | |
| Rough crust | | X | | X | | | | X | | | | X | | | X | | X | |
| Excessive spread | | | | | | | | | | | | | X | | | X | | |

*Figure 8.30  Doughnut problems and their causes*

# CRULLER MIX

| | | |
|---|---|---|
| Sugar | 1 lb | 2 oz |
| Shortening | | 5 oz |
| Salt | | 3/4 oz |
| Vanilla (to taste) | | |
| Mace | | 1/4 oz |
| Eggs (half yolks, half whole eggs) | | 8 oz |
| Milk (1 qt) | 2 lb | |
| Cake flour | 4 lb | |
| Baking powder | | 2 oz |
| | 8 lb | 2 oz |

*Method:* Cream together sugar, shortening, salt, vanilla, and mace. Add eggs and cream. Stir in milk. Sift flour and baking powder together, add to batter, and mix until smooth.

*Scaling instructions:* 1 lb per dozen.

*Frying instructions:* Fry at 370°F.

# BABA AU RHUM

| | | |
|---|---|---|
| Milk (1 pint) | 1 lb | |
| Yeast | | 2 oz |
| Bread flour | | 8 oz |
| Sugar | | 3 oz |
| Eggs | 1 lb | 8 oz |
| Salt | | 1/2 oz |
| Butter, melted | | 8 oz |
| Bread flour | 1 lb | 8 oz |
| Lemon rind, grated (1 lemon) | | |
| | 5 lb | 5 1/2 oz |

*Method:* Make a sponge dough of flour, milk, and yeast. Add remaining ingredients and mix together into a smooth paste. Let this mixture rise for 1 hour, then place in forms. Let rise until double in size and bake. After baking, remove from forms and soak in rum syrup.* Garnish with whipped cream.

*Baking instructions:* 350°F.

*\*Rum syrup:* Boil together 2 qt of water, 2 lb of sugar, the skin from 1 lemon, and 1 cinnamon stick. Add 4 oz of rum.

### Baba au Rhum

Unbaked dough is placed in a greased mold, proofed three times, and baked. The baked baba au rhum is then soaked in rum syrup and either topped or filled with whipped cream and garnished with a cherry.

## SHORTCAKE BISCUITS

| | | |
|---|---|---|
| Cake flour | 2 lb | |
| Salt | | ½ oz |
| Baking powder | | 2 oz |
| Powdered sugar | | 3 oz |
| Shortening or butter | | 12 oz |
| Eggs | | 4 |
| Milk (1 pint) | 1 lb | |
| | 4 lb | 5½ oz |

*Method:* Sift together and blend dry ingredients. Rub in shortening. Beat eggs and milk together and mix. Split the cooked biscuits in half. Place on a dish with the fruit—strawberries or peaches—on top. Cover with the second half of the biscuit, top with whipped cream, and serve.

*Scaling instructions:* 3 dozen 2½-inch biscuits.

*Baking instructions:* 400°F.

## CREPES SUZETTE

| | | |
|---|---|---|
| Cake flour | | 4 oz |
| Sugar | | 2 oz |
| Salt | | ⅛ oz |
| Lemon rind, grated slightly | | |
| (1 lemon) | | |
| Eggs | | 5 oz |
| Butter, melted | | 1 oz |
| Milk | | 8 oz |
| | 1 lb | 4⅛ oz |

*Method:* Melt butter. Sift sugar, salt, and flour together into a bowl. Beat together eggs and milk. Combine egg mixture with dry ingredients and mix until smooth. Add lemon rind and melted butter and mix thoroughly. Heat skillet until moderately hot. Pour in just enough batter to cover bottom of skillet. Tilt skillet or rotate it back and forth to spread batter thinly and evenly. Cook each crepe over medium heat until light brown on bottom side and firm to the touch on top side. Loosen edges with spatula, turn, and brown other side. A slight coating of grease on the skillet may be needed after each crepe.

## S A U C E   F O R   C R E P E S   S U Z E T T E

Orange (1)
Lemon (1)
Sugar (4 lumps)
Butter (1/2 tablespoon)
Curaçao liqueur (1 tablespoon)
Grand Marnier (1 tablespoon)
Cognac (1 tablespoon)

*Method:* Rub sugar against the orange skin. Put them in the sauté pan, add a few drops of lemon juice and the juice of one orange and crush the sugar with a fork. Add the butter and stir well over the fire; then pour in the Curaçao and Grand Marnier. Bring mixture to a boil and remove from the fire. Fold the crepes and place them one by one in the sauce, pour the cognac over them and set on fire. Place the pan on the fire again, bring to a boil, and serve very hot.

## TECHNIQUES FOR PREPARING MERINGUE DESSERTS

Meringues are made principally from egg whites, sugar, and flavoring. The glamorous meringue inspires still another group of exquisite confections.

A meringue is often thought of as a difficult item to make. However, if the formula (Figure 8.32) is followed closely and the basic rules are applied, no difficulty should be encountered and results should be excellent.

It is very important to make sure that all utensils used are clean and free from grease. No traces of yolk should be in the egg whites, and no traces of flour must come in contact with the meringue mixture. There are many variations of meringue shells given on the following pages.

*Figure 8.31  Meringue desserts*

| Method | Ingredients | lb | oz | Cost Per lb | Cost |
|---|---|---|---|---|---|
| 1. Whip together to a stiff peak. | Egg whites | 1 | | | |
| | Granulated sugar | 1 | | | |
| | Flavoring (to taste) | | | | |
| 2. Fold into above mixture, using a minimum amount of motion. | Granulated sugar | 1 | | | |

**TOTAL Yield:** 50 shells

**Scaling Instructions:** tube into desired shapes          **Cost per oz**

**Baking Temperature:** bake dry (about 1 hour)          **Cost per lb**
in 250°F oven

**REMARKS:** For variation, 4 oz granulated
nuts, chocolate bits, or melted chocolate may
be folded in.

*Figure 8.32  Meringue shells—basic formula*

*Figure 8.33  Making meringue shells*

**Rules for Best Results in Making Meringues**

1. Make sure all utensils are free from fat and flour.
2. Use a minimum of handling.
3. Have oven preheated to desired temperature. Meringues should go into oven as soon as made.
4. It is preferable to use paper-lined pans.
5. It is essential that the product is baked dry without browning.

## MERINGUE SHELLS

| | | |
|---|---|---|
| Egg whites | 1 lb | |
| Sugar | 2 lb | |
| Salt | | ¼ oz |
| Vanilla (to taste) | | |
| | 3 lb | ¼ oz |

*Method:* Make a meringue by adding sugar gradually while beating egg whites, salt, and vanilla. Beat until a stiff peak is formed. Make into nests or various shapes by pressing the meringue onto paper-lined pans with a pastry bag. Allow these to dry in a slow oven at 200°F. Serve with ice cream topped with melba sauce. Meringue sticks may be made by forcing the meringue through a pastry tube to form sticks, which are sprinkled with nuts.

*Figure 8.34  French pastries*

*Figure 8.35  Meringue swan components*

### Swans, Baskets, Initials

1. Line a baking sheet with paper. Fit a pastry bag with a plain ¼-inch pastry tube and fill with meringue mixture.
2. Dress out meringue in the shape of question marks to form heads and necks of swans. (See illustration.)
3. To form the wings, make both left and right as shown above.
4. For base of swan, use an oval meringue nest. Let meringues dry in a

*Figure 8.36   Meringue swan*

*Figure 8.37   Meringue basket*

250°F oven for about 1 hour. Then fill base with ice cream or pink whipped cream. Affix meringue head and wings with chocolate or icing.

5. For baskets, make rings or horseshoe shapes for the handle. As a base for the basket, use a round nest filled with whipped cream or ice cream.

*Figure 8.38   Meringue torte*

6. Initials or numerals may be made and used as decorations for cakes and desserts. After dressing out initials or numerals, dry in a 250°F oven for approximately 30 minutes.

**Meringue Torte**

1. Line a baking pan with paper. Trace three circles approximately 8 inches in diameter each. Fit a pastry bag with a plain round tube and fill with meringue mixture.
2. Spiral the meringue on the paper, outlining and filling in the circles.
3. Dry out in 250°F oven for approximately 1 hour. Cool and remove from paper.
4. To serve, alternate layers of meringues with ice cream, whipped cream, fruit, or a combination.

**Schaum Torte**

1. Line a baking pan with paper. Trace four 8-inch circles.
2. Fit a pastry bag with a plain ³/₈-inch tube and fill with meringue mixture.
3. Completely cover one circle with meringue in a spiral effect.
4. Outline two of the circles with meringue approximately 1¹/₂ inches wide and 1 inch thick.

*Figure 8.39  Meringue mushrooms*

5. On the final circle press out a ring of meringue kisses with a star tube. Each kiss must touch the one next to it to form a wreath.
6. Dry in 250°F oven for approximately 1 hour. Cool and remove from paper.
7. Place the solid meringue circle on a cool serving platter.
8. Place the two outlined circles on top of the solid circle.
9. Fold 1 pint sliced strawberries that have been soaked in liqueur into 1 pint heavy cream that has been whipped.
10. Fill the meringue shell with this mixture and place the wreath of meringue kisses on top. Garnish with a whole strawberry.

## Meringue Mushrooms

1. Line a baking sheet with paper. Fit a pastry bag with a ³⁄₈-inch round tube and fill with meringue mixture.
2. Dress out several stems about 2 inches high. Also dress out an equal number of 1-inch round caps.
3. Sprinkle caps with cocoa powder or cinnamon.
4. Bake in 250°F oven for approximately 30 minutes. Cool. Affix caps to stems with chocolate icing. Mushrooms may be served as a garnish for ice cream or as a petit four.

## Meringue Glacé

1. Line a baking pan with paper. Fit a pastry bag with a star tube and fill with meringue mixture. Dress out rosettes or ovals.
2. Sprinkle with fine granulated sugar, and follow instructions for meringue shells.
3. To serve, press a meringue rosette or oval on each side of a scoop of ice cream. Garnish with whipped cream.

*Figure 8.40   Meringue nest or shells*

*Figure 8.41   Meringue pie shell*

## Meringue Nest or Shells

1. Line a baking sheet with paper. Using a pastry bag and a plain ³/₈-inch pastry tube filled with meringue mixture, dress out round or oval nests 3 to 4 inches in diameter and approximately 1 inch high. Space apart on the sheet pan.
2. Sprinkle these shells with fine granulated sugar.
3. Bake in 250°F oven for approximately 1 hour. (Meringues will peel freely from paper when dried out sufficiently. Meringues of this type should dry out without browning.)
4. To serve, fill with fruit, whipped cream, or mousse. Garnish with whipped cream or sauce.

*Figure 8.42  Meringue kisses*

### Meringue Pie Shell

1. Butter and flour a pie pan.
2. Fit a pastry bag with a ³/₈-inch plain tube and fill with meringue mixture. Starting from the center of pie plate, spiral the meringue all the way to the side and top of pie plate. Make meringue about ³/₄ inch thick.
4. Dry out in a 250°F oven for approximately 1½ hours. Loosen from paper and cool.
5. Many interesting and attractive fillings may be used for this shell.

### Meringue Kisses

1. Fit a pastry bag with a star tube; fill with meringue mixture.
2. Dress out small, interesting shapes. (As a variation, fold granulated nuts or chocolate into meringue mixture before dressing out.)
3. Dry in a 250°F oven for approximately 25 minutes.

### Meringue Variations

In addition to the variations already described, meringues can be made into many other shapes including round, oval, boats, hearts, shamrocks, animals and cookies.

Many different fillings may be used. Among the most popular are whipped cream, ice cream, fruit fillings, or tart lemon filling (two parts lemon filling with one part whipped cream folded together).


## MERINGUES

There are many desserts and pies that can be made to look more attractive with the addition of a meringue topping.

Three types of meringue are generally used:

## COMMON MERINGUE

| Egg whites | 1 lb |
|---|---|
| Sugar | 2 lb |
| | 3 lb |

*Method:* Beat the egg whites and gradually add the sugar. After all the sugar has been added, beat to the desired consistency.

## ITALIAN MERINGUE

| Egg whites | 1 lb | |
|---|---|---|
| Sugar | 2 lb | |
| Water | | 8 oz |
| | 3 lb | 8 oz |

*Method:* Beat the egg whites lightly. Cook the sugar and water to 244°F and add gradually to beaten egg whites in a slow, steady stream. Continue beating until the desired consistency is reached.

## SWISS MERINGUE

| Egg whites | 1 lb |
|---|---|
| Sugar | 2 lb |
| | 3 lb |

*Method:* Heat the sugar and egg whites in a bain marie or double boiler and whip until they are very warm. Then place in the machine and beat to the proper consistency.

*Figure 8.43   Chocolate boxes*

## ASSORTED PASTRIES

### Chocolate Boxes

Heat sweet chocolate, spread it thinly on a papered pan, and let it cool. Cut it into 2-inch squares. Do the same with white chocolate. Split cake into two strips 2 inches wide, spread a layer of jelly or butter cream icing on one strip, and sandwich the two layers together. The cake is then cut into 2-inch squares and the sides are masked with chocolate icing. The chocolate squares are then affixed to the sides of the cake squares. The boxes are then topped with butter cream or chocolate icing and garnished with a cherry or pistachio nut.

*Figure 8.44   Franchipan pastries*

## Franchipan Pastries

Various cuts of Franchipan cake are enrobed in fondant icing and then finished with the desired decoration.

## Napoleons

Take three strips of baked puff pastry, about 3½ inches wide, and spread pastry cream between the strips. Then, spread warm (about 98°) fondant icing over the top and decorate with lines of contrasting color. Finally, cut the finished product into slices.

## Jelly Roll Fantasy

Cake is cut into 2½-inch squares and topped with butter cream icing. Jelly roll, filled with mocha, jelly, or lemon filling, is cut into slices and each slice cut into fourths. The pieces are rearranged to form a square. These squares are placed on the cake and the centers are filled with jelly, chocolate, or white fondant.

1. Napoleon.

2. Fondant on top

3. Chocolate icing with piping tube.

4. With dull edge of knife draw lines across top as shown.

5. Reverse direction of knife stroke. Lines are drawn between those previously made in part 4.

6. Finished design.

*Figure 8.45 Napoleons*

## Cream Puff Baskets and Swans

Cream puff baskets and swans both use the bottom half of the cream puff shell as their base. The swan's neck and the basket's handle are separate pieces of shaped and baked pâte à chou dough. The wings of the swan are

*Figure 8.46 Cream horns and jelly roll fantasy*

made from halves of the baked shell's top. The finished basket or swan is filled with cream, garnished with a cherry, and sprinkled with powdered sugar. The cream puff shells themselves can be dipped in white or chocolate fondant icings and filled with pastry cream.

### Éclairs

The éclair shells are baked and then either filled with pastry cream and dipped in chocolate or white fondant icing or, split, dipped in chocolate or white fondant icing, and then filled with whipped cream.

### Fruit Tartlets

Roll pie crust or short pastry about 1/8-inch thick and cut with a pastry cutter to 41/4-inch diameter. Press into tartlet pan and trim. Fill pastry 3/4 full with rock salt, beans, or rice during baking of shell. After baking, fill shell 1/2 full with pastry cream and cover with sponge cake about 1/4 inch thick and 11/2 inches in diameter. Fruits such as peach, strawberries, pineapple, bing cherries (canned or fresh), pears, apricots, bananas, grapes, and blueberries can be used as topping. After the fruit has been put over the sponge cake, cover with hot apricot glaze.

*Figure 8.47   Cream puff baskets, cream puff swans, and éclairs*

### Franchipan Tartlets

Put 2 oz of Franchipan mixture into a tart pan and bake. Cut out, *not* to the bottom, a section from the center of the tart. Fill tart with pastry cream and sprinkle with powdered sugar. Cutout sections are topped with currant jelly and put on top of the tart.

### Parfaits

Parfaits are combinations of various colored and flavored ice creams, fruits, and sauces, topped with whipped cream. They should be served in tall, narrow glasses.

To make a parfait, place one spoon of crushed fruit in the parfait glass. Add a dipper of ice cream and cover with a spoonful of crushed fruit. Add another dipper of ice cream and cover again with crushed fruit. Add another dipper of ice cream and cover again with a spoonful of crushed fruit. Now cover with a spoonful of nuts in syrup and top with whipped cream. Decorate with a piece of fruit or nut.

Pour one or two tablespoons of sauce or syrup into a parfait glass. Place the ice cream in the glass and force it down into the syrup, which will work

*Figure 8.48   Fruit tartlets*

*Figure 8.49   Parfait*

itself into a spiral around the inside of the glass. Top with whipped cream. Serve immediately or place in the freezer until serving time.

A few variations into which this popular dessert may be made are:

*Melba:* Vanilla ice cream with melba sauce
*Java:* Coffee ice cream with chocolate sauce
*Nesselrode:* Vanilla ice cream with Nesselrode mixture

*Figure 8.50   Coupe*

*Rainbow:* Vanilla, strawberry, and chocolate ice cream with strawberry
   sauce
*Strawberry:* Vanilla ice cream with strawberry sauce
*Butterscotch:* Vanilla ice cream with butterscotch sauce
*Chocolate:* Chocolate ice cream with chocolate sauce
*Pineapple mint:* Lemon sherbert with pineapple mint sauce

## Coupe

In French, this word means "cup" or "goblet." It is also used to describe a
dessert served in these dishes.

Coupes are made with ice cream, sherbet or ices, fruits and spirits, whipped
cream, and sauces of various kinds. They are served in tall stemmed glasses
or champagne glasses.

To make a coupe, place sauce or fruit in the glass. Add a dipper of ice
cream, and cover with a sauce of fruit and spirits. Decorate with whipped
cream.

*Strawberry Coupe:* Vanilla ice cream, strawberries, and whipped cream
*Coupe St. Jacques:* Maraschino, fresh fruit salad, raspberry and lemon
   sherbet
*Coupe Helen:* Crème de menthe, black bing cherries, ice cream,
   whipped cream, and brandy
*Pineapple Coupe:* Ice cream, pineapple, whipped cream, and kirsch
*Coupe Melba:* Vanilla ice cream, peaches, and Melba sauce
*Coupe aux Marrons:* Candied chestnuts, vanilla ice cream, and whipped
   cream

*Figure 8.51   Franchipan tartlets*

## TECHNIQUES FOR ICE CREAM DESSERTS

Ice cream is one of the nation's favorite desserts. Coupes, parfaits, mousses, oven-browned ice cream desserts, and bombes are only a few of the many desserts that can be made with ice cream. Because elaborate-appearing ice cream desserts are often easy to prepare, they will not put undue strain on the production department.

Here is a collection of ice cream dessert variations that will glamorize any menu.

### Baked Alaska Grand Success

Cut out center of an 8-inch sponge cake, and fill cavity with well-drained bing cherries (canned). Top with layer of ice cream; add the piece cut from center of cake. Cover with meringue, making a pyramid effect. Brown and top with apricot halves. (Figures 8.45 through 8.49 show preparation of baked Alaska grand success.)

*Figure 8.52  Step 1: to make baked Alaska grand success, cut center from an 8-inch sponge cake; fill the cavity with well-drained bing cherries (kirsch may be added for flavoring)*

*Figure 8.53  Step 2: top sponge cake and cherries with a layer of hard ice cream; on top of the layer of ice cream, place the piece of sponge cake previously cut from the center of the cake*

## Cantaloupe Alaska

Cut cantaloupe in two. Remove seeds. Fill cavity with ice cream. Top with meringue. Brown meringue and serve.

*Figure 8.54  Step 3: cover the entire dessert with meringue, swirling around the sides (because the center slice of sponge cake is smaller than the base, you will have a pyramid effect)*

## Orange Surprise

Place a small piece of sponge cake on the bottom of an orange rind cup. Add a scoop of ice cream. Cover with meringue. Brown.

## Coconut Tropical Dessert

Use half-shell of a coconut with a paper cut as a liner. Start with fruit as a base (sliced banana or pineapple, etc.). Add ice cream. Top with meringue and brown, or top with whipped cream and shredded coconut or macadamia nuts.

## Fresh Pineapple Delight

Quarter fresh pineapple. Remove core. Add small piece of sponge cake. Top with ice cream. Cover with meringue. Brown. This dessert also can be made with a pear half instead of pineapple.

## Chocolate Ice Cream Cups

To chocolate shelled cups, add ice cream, whipped cream and top with nuts.

## Fruit Mousse

A fruit flavored mousse should be garnished with the same fruit used as purée in the recipe.

*Figure 8.55 Step 4: top the pyramid with additional meringue, using a pastry tube; illustrating this step is Joe Amendola, Bakery Chef at The Culinary Institute of America*

### Snow Princess

Top sponge cake with a scoop of ice cream and place a small doll (the princess) in the center of the ice cream. Add whipped cream around the base of the sponge cake. Garnish with cherries.

*Figure 8.56   Step 5: place baked Alaska in the oven long enough to brown the meringue; top with apricot halves*

### Banana Surprise

Make a cream éclair into the shape of a banana. Slit éclair in half. Add pastry cream or ice cream and half a banana. Top with chocolate sauce and nuts.

### Ladyfinger Ice Cream

Top sponge cake with ice cream and place ladyfingers around the ice cream. Top with whipped cream and cherry. Garnish with sauce around base.

### Appareil à Bombe

Appareil à bombe is a base made for mousse or biscuit (bisque) glacé. It consists primarily of egg yolks, sugar, and water and is prepared as follows:

1.  Mix 3 lb sugar and 1 lb water and cook at 240°F until it reaches the soft ball stage.
2.  Place 24 egg yolks in a mixer and beat with a whip at medium speed.
3.  Pour cooked sugar and water mixture slowly on top of eggs while they are being beaten, and beat until cold. When a creamy consistency has been reached, remove from mixer and place in refrigerator until ready for use. This paste will keep for a week or longer under refrigeration.
4.  When ready to use base in making mousses, biscuits glacé, etc., fold $1/2$ lb of base mixture into each quart of whipped cream. Add liquor, fruit, etc., as needed for specific dessert.

## Biscuit Tortoni

To the basic appareil à bombe mixture, add 1 oz rum or brandy and 4 oz crushed macaroons. Mix together and fill tortoni cups. Use a star tube. Sprinkle with crushed macaroons, top with a maraschino cherry, and freeze.

## Mousse

Mousses are frozen whipped ice cream desserts of various flavors. The identifying flavor (chocolate, strawberry, mocha, etc.) is added to the base and whipped cream mixture. It is then put in brick type molds and frozen. For serving, cut into slices or serve as larger pieces decorated with whipped cream and fruits and topped with a sauce.

## Biscuit Glacé

Biscuits glacé are made from the same basic mixture as mousses. These desserts are frozen in paper soufflé cups or cases and are served in the same containers in which they are frozen. The dessert is usually decorated to harmonize with the flavor of the mixture.

## Ice Cream Bombes

Originally ice cream bombes were spherical or dome shaped, hence the name bombe.

Today ice cream bombes vary in shape, but their contents remain basically the same.

The traditional method of making ice cream bombes is to place the mixture in a mold and freeze it in ice and rock salt. However, today's advanced freezing facilities make this unnecessary.

Although any shape of mold may be used, spherical molds have an interesting and attractive appearance. Two attractive shapes of bombe molds are shown in Figure 8.58.

To make an ice cream bombe, line the mold with ice cream, ice, sherbet, mousse, fruit or nuts and candy, or a combination of two or three of these ingredients. Freeze.

## Unmolding Bombes

To unmold ice cream bombes, dip the mold quickly into hot water. Dry the mold and place upside down on a cold platter. Remove mold.

*Figure 8.57  Mousses, biscuits glacé, biscuit tortoni; variations from appareil à bombe mixture include chocolate and strawberry mousse heart* (top left and right); *Neopolitan mousse* (center); *chocolate-vanilla, coffee walnut, and mocha biscuit glacés* (lower left); *biscuit tortoni* (lower right)

### Slicing and Serving Bombes

An ice cream bombe should be garnished and served immediately after unmolding. The bombe is usually topped with whipped cream. Additional garnishing is up to the ingenuity of the chef.

To slice ice cream bombes, use a silver knife dipped in hot water.

### Strawberry Bombe

Mask a bombe mold with strawberry ice cream. Make a second lining of lemon ice. Fill with strawberries that have been soaked in kirsch. Freeze.

### Bombe Carmen

Mask a bombe mold with vanilla ice cream about ½ inch thick. Fill the center with a raspberry mousse. Freeze.

*Figure 8.58 Ice cream bombes: traditional ice cream bombes are made in spherical or dome-shaped molds as shown at right, but many different shapes of molds are now available, and decoration is up to the ingenuity of the chef.*

*Figure 8.59 Sundae*

*Figure 8.60   Banana split*

### Sundae

To make a sundae, place 1/2 oz of crushed, sliced, or whole fruit into a dish. Add two dippers of ice cream and surround the ice cream with 1 oz of crushed, sliced, or whole fruit. Add nuts and top with whipped cream and a piece of fruit.

### Banana Split

To make a banana split, split a banana in half, lengthwise, with the peel on. Place one half on each side of the dish, flat side down, and remove the peel. Place three dippers of ice cream on the banana halves using vanilla in the center and other flavors on each side. Cover each dipper of ice cream with a different topping, 1/2 oz of each kind. Garnish the top and between the ice cream dippers with whipped cream. Sprinkle on nuts and add a piece of fruit.

### Milk Shake

A milk shake is made by putting 6 oz of milk into a chilled cup and adding two dippers of ice cream and 1 1/2 oz of syrup. Mix thoroughly and rapidly and pour into a serving glass.

### Ice Cream Soda

To make an ice cream soda, place 1 1/2 oz of syrup into a 14-oz glass. Stir a spoonful of ice cream or 1 1/2 oz of coffee cream into the syrup. Fill the glass 3/4 full with carbonated water and float two dippers of ice cream. Mix gently and add carbonated water to fill the glass. Top with whipped cream.

### Spumoni

Spumoni is an Italian molded ice cream with an outer layer of custard containing chopped almonds and an inner filling made with heavy cream, sugar, cherries, and candied orange peel.

To make spumoni, place chocolate ice cream into a mold to form the outer layer. Place strawberry ice cream on the chocolate ice cream to form the second layer. Repeat with vanilla ice cream. Fill the cavity with whipped cream or mousse with nut and fruit mixture. Freeze, unmold, and serve.

*Figure 8.61    Cassata*

### Cassata

To make cassata, place pistachio ice cream into a melon-shaped mold to form the outer layer. Place strawberry ice cream into the mold to form the second layer, and repeat with chocolate ice cream. Fill the cavity with mousse or whipped cream with pistachio nuts. Freeze, unmold, and serve.

### Ice Cream Pie

Place ice cream into a prebaked pie shell (usually two different flavors are used), decorate the top with whipped cream, and serve with crushed strawberries. These pies may be made and then stored in a freezer until serving time.

### Snowball

Take a large scoop of ice cream and roll it in macaroon coconut. Put some chocolate sauce on a cold plate and place the ice cream ball in the center.

### Peach Melba

Cut a round of sponge cake and place a scoop of ice cream in the center. Place a second round of sponge cake over the ice cream to form a sandwich. Place half a peach over this. Pour melba sauce over all and garnish with whipped cream and sliced toasted almonds.

### Meringue Glacé

Place a scoop of ice cream on a cold plate with a meringue kiss on each side. Pour melba or strawberry sauce over the ice cream.

*Figure 8.62   Peach Melba*

*Figure 8.63   Meringue glacé*

### Frozen Éclair

Fill an eclair shell with vanilla ice cream. Top this with chocolate or butter-scotch sauce. Garnish with whipped cream and serve.

### Ice Cream Puff

Stuff a cream puff shell with vanilla ice cream. Top this with chocolate or butterscotch sauce. Garnish with whipped cream and serve.

### Baked Alaska

Cut a ½-inch-thick sponge cake into an oval shape. Remove a portion of the center and place on a silver platter. Have on hand a meringue mixture. Fill the oval with vanilla ice cream, molding high as for a dome, and cover

*Figure 8.64   Ice cream puff*

*Figure 8.65   Baked Alaska*

quickly with the meringue mixture. Decorate with this same mixture, forcing it through a pastry bag. Dust with sugar and bake at 450°F. Serve immediately.

**Pear Hélène**

Place a piece of sponge cake on a serving dish. Top it with a scoop of ice cream. Place a pear half on the ice cream. Cover this with chocolate sauce. Garnish with whipped cream and serve.

*Figure 8.66   Pear Hélène*

# CHARLOTTE À L'AMERICAINE

| | | |
|---|---|---|
| Apples, sliced | 1 lb | |
| Butter | | 2 oz |
| Apricot sauce | | 4 oz |
| Pineapple, crushed | | 8 oz |
| Bananas, sliced | | 8 oz |
| Lemon rind (1 lemon) | | |
| Kirsch | | 1 oz |
| | 2 lb | 7 oz |

*Method:* Heat butter and add apples and toss them over a good fire until tender. Add the apricot sauce and simmer a few more minutes, then fold in the pineapple, bananas, and lemon rind. Remove from fire. Add kirsch and blend in. Serves 8.

Butter a charlotte mold, 4 inches high and 4½ inches in diameter. Cover the bottom with thin, round slices of white sandwich bread ⅛ inch thick (use stale bread, if possible). Arrange slices around the bottom and in the center so that they slightly overlap one another, carefully dipping them as needed in clarified butter. Then, cut some ⅛-inch-thick slices of bread into 1-inch strips, having them the same height as the mold. Dip them in butter and place them upright and slightly overlapping one another around the inner side of the mold. Fill the mold with the fruit mixture and bake at 375°F for 1 hour or until the bread appears golden brown. Remove from oven and let cool. Pour over it a fruit sauce with kirsch and serve some whipped cream separately.

*Apple charlotte:* Use 2 lb sliced apples in place of bananas and pineapple.

*Figure 8.67   Charlotte royal*

# VANILLA BAVARIAN CREAM

| | | |
|---|---|---|
| Gelatin | | 1 ½ oz |
| Water | | 12 oz |
| Egg yolks (12) | | 8 oz |
| Granulated sugar | | 8 oz |
| Milk (1 qt) | 2 lb | |
| Vanilla bean | | |
| Whipped cream (1 qt) | 2 lb | |
| | 5 lb | 13½ oz |

*Method:* Soak gelatin in cold water. Beat yolks and 4 oz of sugar until thick and fluffy. Place milk and vanilla in a saucepan, and bring to a boil. Remove from heat, and pour slowly over the yolk mixture, stirring and bleeding all ingredients rapidly. Add soaked gelatin; stir well to dissolve into the milk. Place in a round bowl over crushed ice or in the refrigerator, stirring from time to time to expedite the cooling process. When yolk mixture begins to set and thicken, fold in the whipped cream and mix thoroughly. Pour into prepared molds or serving dishes.

*Yield:* 18 individual servings.

*Figure 8.68    Charlotte Russe*

# SPONGE ROULADES

| | | |
|---|---|---|
| Egg yolks (30) | 1 lb | 5 oz |
| Sugar | | 6 oz |
| Egg whites (30) | 1 lb | 14 oz |
| Sugar | 1 lb | 2 oz |
| Cake flour | | 11 oz |
| Cornstarch | | 8 oz |
| | 5 lb | 14 oz |

*Method:* Whip egg yolks and sugar to a light foam. Whip egg whites and sugar to a soft peak. Fold by hand the two mixtures. Sift cake flour and cornstarch and fold into the mixture. Bake at 375°F for approximately ten minutes. After baking, spread with jelly and roll into a spiral.

*Yield:* 4–5 sheets.

### Charlotte Russe

Line the sides of a charlotte mold with the required number of ladyfingers, previously trimmed. Then fill the mold with either Bavarian or whipped cream. Refrigerate until set. Unmold, decorate with whipped cream, and serve. These are quite often made as individual desserts in small paper cups or containers.

### Charlotte Royal

Line a charlotte mold with thin slices of jelly roll, and fill with either Bavarian or whipped cream. Unmold, decorate with whipped cream, and serve.

*Figure 8.69   Charlotte royal*

## RICE IMPERATRIC E

| | | |
|---|---|---|
| Water (1 pint) | 1 lb | |
| Raspberry gelatin | | 4 oz |
| Rice, blanched | 2 lb | |
| Milk (1 qt) | 2 lb | |
| Salt | | 1/2 oz |
| Vanilla (to taste) | | |
| Gelatin | | 1 oz |
| Sugar | | 8 oz |
| Heavy cream (1 qt) | 2 lb | |
| Maraschino cherries, chopped | | 8 oz |
| | 8 lb | 5 1/2 oz |

*Method:* Dissolve gelatin in hot water. Place 1/2 inch on bottom of mold to be used and allow to set. Place rice, milk, salt, vanilla, gelatin, and sugar in a pot and cook and simmer for approximately 10 minutes. Allow to cool and set. Whip cream and fold in with mixture that has been set. Fold cherries into mixture, and place into molds or forms that have the gelatin set on bottom. Place in refrigerator until set. Unmold by setting forms in warm water and place on serving plates.

# FRUIT CONDÉ

| | | |
|---|---|---|
| Milk (1 pint) | 1 lb | |
| Rice, blanched | 1 lb | |
| Salt | | ¼ oz |
| Sugar | | 4 oz |
| Gelatin | | ½ oz |
| Heavy cream (1 pint) | 1 lb | |
| | 3 lb | 4¾ oz |

*Method:* Place all ingredients except cream in a pot and simmer for approximately 10 minutes and allow to cool and set. Whip cream and fold in with mixture that has been set. Place this mixture in a large or small charlotte mold and refrigerate until mixture is set. When set, unmold on a dish and place assorted fruit on top of rice mixture. Brush top of fruit with a hot apricot sauce and serve.

# PEACH CONDÉ

Prepare above rice mixture and place in a large, small, or individual charlotte mold and let stand and refrigerate until mixture is set. When set, unmold on a dish, place peach halves on top of rice, brush all over with hot apricot sauce, and serve.

*Variations:* Figs, strawberries, pears, and apples can be served in place of peaches.

# BAVARIAN CREAMS II.
# AND CHARLOTTES

| | | |
|---|---|---|
| Milk (1 qt) | 2 lb | |
| Egg yolks (6) | | |
| Sugar | | 8 oz |
| Gelatin (plain) | | 1/2 oz |
| Heavy cream (1 pint) | 1 lb | |
| | 3 lb | 8 1/2 oz |

*Method:* Heat milk. Heat together yolks, sugar, and gelatin and add to milk, but do not boil. Whip cream and fold into mixture after it has cooled and started to thicken. Place into a mold or cup and allow to set until firm. Unmold and serve with sauce. Serves 12.

*Variations:* Coffee, chocolate, walnut, maple, or liqueur of any flavor. The mixture is also suitable for preparing the various chilled charlotte desserts such as charlotte royal, charlotte russe, strawberry charlotte, etc.

# STRAWBERRY CHARLOTTE

Line the bottom of a plain charlotte mold with strawberry jelly; then line the sides with ladyfingers and fill the center with a strawberry Bavarian cream mixture. When set, unmold the charlotte on a cold dish and decorate or garnish with whipped cream and strawberries. Variations can be made by substituting peach, raspberry, apricot, or other fruits for strawberries.

# A P P E N D I X

## SUGAR COOKING

The ideal proportion of sugar to water is three parts sugar and one part water. These should be placed in a copper or stainless steel pot and stirred until the mass comes to a boil.

The sides of the pot may be brushed with water to clean them of any sugar crystals. Or the pot may be covered while the syrup is boiling, allowing the steam to wash down the sides. This is an important step in the early stages.

Continue to cook the syrup until it reaches the proper degree. Expert confectioners usually judge the degree of the syrup by dipping the index finger into cold water and then immediately dipping the same finger into the boiling syrup. This method is definitely not recommended for a novice because of the danger involved; a candy thermometer should be used. (When not in actual use, place the candy thermometer in a jar of warm water near the stove, eliminating the possibility of breakage, which often occurs when a cold thermometer is placed in hot syrup.)

The following chart indicates the boiling stages and the temperature readings for each stage. Because it only takes a few degrees to bring the syrup to another stage, temperature control is very important. It is also important to remember that temperatures in the chart below may vary because of differences in humidity and altitude.

| Stages | Temperatures |
|---|---|
| Thread | 230°–235°F |
| Soft ball | 240°–245°F |
| Ball | 250°–255°F |
| Hard ball | 260°–265°F |
| Small crack | 270°–275°F |
| Crack | 275°–280°F |
| Hard crack | 285°–315°F |
| Caramel | 325°–350°F |

The proportion of sugar and water varies as the cooking proceeds:

| Temperature of Water and Sugar | Percent of Sugar Present | Percent of Water Present |
|---|---|---|
| 212.7°F | 10 | 90 |
| 213.8°F | 30 | 70 |
| 215.6°F | 50 | 50 |
| 223.7°F | 70 | 30 |
| 225.2°F | 75 | 25 |
| 238.8°F | 85 | 15 |
| 243.8°F | 87 | 13 |
| 249.5°F | 89 | 11 |
| 252.7°F | 90 | 10 |

## Rock Sugar or Soufflé Sugar

Rock sugar is quite simple to make. It is appropriate for use for rock forma-
tions, bases for lighthouses made of sugar, etc. Rock sugar should be cooked
in an extra-large kettle, because the mixture rises and foams considerably.
Have a wooden or cardboard box available to pour the mixture into when it
is ready. If a wooden box is used, it should be lined with paper. A cake box
12 × 12 × 6 inches would be adequate for the amount of mixture in the
following recipe:

| | | |
|---|---|---|
| Granulated sugar | 3 lb | |
| Water (1 pint) | 1 lb | |
| Corn syrup | | 5 oz |
| Egg whites (1) | | |

*Method:* Cook sugar and water to 280°F and remove from the heat. Whip
together whites and syrup and add to heated mixture. Stir slowly with a
wooden paddle. The mixture will bubble and foam and then appear to drop.

Stir continuously until it rises for the second time. When the mixture starts to settle the second time, pour it into the box and it will rise. Allow it to set until firm. It will be porous and can be broken off into the desired sized pieces and stuck together with royal icing.

## MARZIPAN

Marzipan is a candy that has a definite almond flavor. It is adaptable to many uses. It may be molded or hand-carved into fruits, vegetables, animal figures, etc., or it may be used as a topping for cookies and cakes.

When using a mold with marzipan, it is best to dust the mold first with confectioners' sugar to prevent sticking. Remove the marzipan from the mold immediately and allow it to dry.

When colored appropriately with dry or liquid coloring, marzipan can be very attractive. There are a number of recipes for marzipan, but the one below seems the most satisfactory.

| | |
|---|---|
| Almond paste | 1 lb |
| Confectioners' sugar | 1 lb |

*Method:* Rub together until fine. Either fondant icing, egg whites, or a simple syrup may be used to bring this mixture to a fine, firm consistency.

Marzipan is a very versatile confection and an interesting medium for many confectionery creations. The following will give some ideas.

Begin with the proper tools: a plain or ribbed rolling pin, tweezers, bone or wooden sculpturing tools, and a blowtorch for the browning effect on some pieces. Other tools can be adapted as needed, such as a light bulb to give a curl to a flower petal.

Figure A.1 shows an unusual picture frame with a floral design, made entirely with marzipan of various colors. The borders are made separately from flat or ribbed marzipan (by using the plain or ribbed rolling pins) rolled about a cylinder. The cylindrical pieces are then decorated with the tweezers and sculpturing tools. The antique effect is accomplished with the blowtorch. The flowers and other designs are made by cutting and putting together small pieces of colored marzipan.

### Specialty Cakes

Specialty cakes for Thanksgiving and other holidays can be made from marzipan by using the same basic principles illustrated here. To make an ear of corn, for example, cut a sheet cake into oblong pieces and cover them with

*Figure A.1   A picture frame made of marzipan*

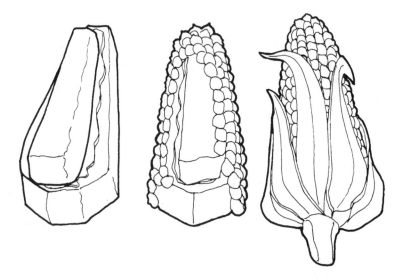

*Figure A.2   Ears of corn made of sheet cake and marzipan*

dots of yellow butter cream icing to achieve the corn effect. The husk is made by rolling out marzipan, cutting it, and laying it in the cake in the proper position.

Another possibility for Thanksgiving is a turkey. This is made by cutting a sheet cake into the general shape of a roast turkey and masking it with butter cream icing. The entire cake is then covered with a thin neutral marzipan to give the turkey effect. Finally, the surface of the marzipan is covered with a caramel-colored glaze to give the finished cake the roasted effect that a turkey would have. As a finishing touch, cut fringes in a paper cylinder and put it on the legs of the "turkey."

## Blown and Pulled Sugar

The sugar centerpieces shown in Figures A.3 through A.5 are the work of Charles Camarano, a master pastry cook and candy maker. These attractive decorations are made of cooked sugar that has been pulled and blown. Mr. Camarano's techniques are described here.

| | | |
|---|---|---|
| Granulated sugar | 5 lb | |
| Water (1 pint) | 1 lb | |
| Cream of tartar | | 1/4 oz |
| Salad oil (for use on marble slab) | | |
| Assorted paste coloring | | |

*Recipe and method of cooking sugar:* Place 5 lb granulated cane sugar and 1 pint of water in a heavy pot, preferably copper, over medium heat. When sugar and water begin to boil, add 1/4 oz cream of tartar that has been melted in 1 tablespoon of water. Turn heat as high as possible so that the sugar cooks fast. Wash the sides of the pot occasionally with a wet brush to prevent granulation around the pot. When the candy thermometer reaches 318°F, pour sugar over a lightly oiled marble slab. If various colors are desired, simply pour the sugar onto the slab in separate quantities and color as desired. At first the sugar will appear transparent.

After the sugar has been cooked and poured onto the marble slab, work it by turning the edges into the center from time to time to keep the edges as soft and pliable as the center. When the sugar begins to hold its shape, pull several times until its texture is silky and shiny. If the sugar is pulled too much, it will lose its gloss and get a waxy appearance. Place the sugar on a canvas in front of the batch warmer to keep it soft and pliable. The sugar is now ready to work with.

## Fruit and Novelties

To make the pear tree shown in Figure A.3, the sugar was blown, much as a glassblower blows glass. A small round metal tube is inserted into a round ball of yellow-colored pulled sugar. Pull the sugar up and around the metal

*Figure A.3   A pear tree made of blown and pulled sugar*

tube, then blow through the tube very gently so that the sugar will expand evenly. Pull the neck a little to form the elongated upper section. To keep the fragile sugar from breaking or cooling too fast, place your hands gently around it to keep it warm. After it is blown to the desired size or until it is quite thin, place the object in front of a cooling fan until it becomes firm; otherwise it will distort and collapse.

After the piece has been shaped and cooled, cut off the neck with a hot

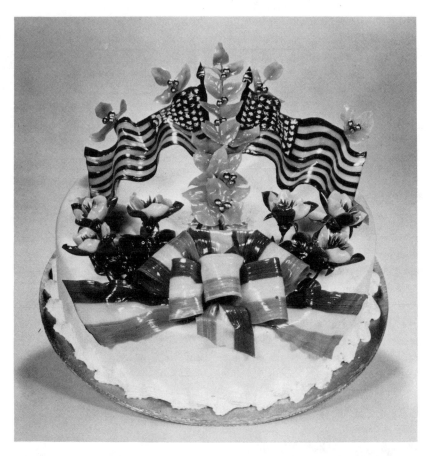

*Figure A.4   A patriotic ribbon-and-bow design of blown and pulled sugar*

knife by cutting through the sugar next to the metal tube. Finish by placing a stem and leaf on top of the pear.

Color tone is applied by dipping a 1-inch brush into red paste coloring and brushing on the tone desired. This same procedure is used in making various fruits and vegetables, vases, etc., which are to be very thin and hollow inside.

## Ribbons and Bows

Long strips of sugar are pulled for ribbons and bows. The width is determined by the size of the article or basket on which it is to be used. The sugar is pulled until it is very thin, making the width as uniform as possible. The sugar ribbon must not be pulled in a cool area; work only in front of the batch warmer.

To make bows, cut the ribbons into desired lengths. Bend the lengths so that the two ends meet with a loop between. Each bow or loop is made individually and is formed while the sugar is pliable enough to be shaped. The loops are stood up straight in front of the cooling fan on the marble slab so that they hold their shape. The loops needed, as well as the two long strips to be used as streamers, should all be made before putting them together.

To form the complete bow, take several loops and melt the cut edges over a bunsen burner; then attach each loop to form the bow.

## Multicolored Ribbon

Color half of the sugar one color and leave the other half plain white. Pull the white sugar into a long but not too thin strip, and lay it in front of the batch warmer. Pull the colored sugar the same way and lay it so that the edge just covers the edge of the white strip. Press down on the two pieces of sugar so that they stick together, making one wide strip. Cut the strip in half again, and place one half so that it just overlaps the edge of the other half. This will make eight strips of alternating colors. This process may be repeated to make as many color strips as needed. Warm the strip evenly and then pull until the ribbon is long and thin. Place it on a canvas to cool and become firm. With a hot knife, heated over a flame, cut the strip into desired lengths. To reshape or bend, place the strip in front of the batch warmer to make it pliable before placing it on the article.

## Pulled Sugar Basket Weaving

Basket weaving requires a board, either round or oval, which has an uneven number of holes drilled into the board at an angle (for instance, from 19 to 25 holes, but always an uneven number). Wooden or metal skewers, the desired height of the basket, are then placed into the holes. The board and skewers should be lightly greased.

The sugar is woven by pulling it into the shape of a cord and weaving it in and out of the skewers until the desired height is reached. At this point, the skewers are removed and replaced with skewers made from pulled sugar. The basket is finished with a double-twisted strand of pulled sugar around the top and bottom of the basket.

The handle is made by drawing a rather stiff piece of wire through a piece of pulled sugar. This action coats the wire, which may then be curved and shaped to form a handle of desired form. Attach handle to the basket and decorate as desired.

The finished products should be kept in an airtight container. By using silica gel (with indicator) or rock lime in the container, moisture will be kept to a minimum and the sugar work will be preserved.

## CRYSTAL SUGAR

Crystal sugar work might be considered a preliminary lesson to pulled sugar work. Crystal sugar is less time-consuming than pulled sugar; consequently, the finished product is ready faster and is of a durability that adapts to nut or candy dishes, floral baskets, etc.

Crystal sugar is cooked and prepared in the same way as pulled sugar. After cooking, it is poured onto a marble slab to form a round flat disc of the desired size. Allowed to cool sufficiently, it then is placed on a greased or lightly oiled inverted vase or bowl. Additional shaping around the bowl is necessary.

When the crystal sugar has cooled and set firmly, it is removed, set right side up, and finished with decorating touches using royal icing, pulled sugar flowers, or leaves. The result is a beautiful sugar piece that does not require the tedious work of the woven basket, etc., of the pulled sugar pieces.

## GUM PASTE

Gum paste, or pastillage as it is sometimes called, is used for making model display pieces from the skyscrapers to the smallest abode, and from simple baskets to the most intricate masterpieces. Gum paste is also excellent for making various flowers.

Before attempting to produce a showpiece of this kind, careful consideration should be given to plans, outlines, and photographic patterns.

Molding gum paste is easy if the mold is clean and dry and dusted lightly with cornstarch. It is wise to use a marble slab for rolling or cutting out the gum paste into various shapes; this will guarantee smooth pieces. Always be sure the slab is clean and free from dry pieces of gum paste before using. The paste must also be worked smooth before rolling. Cutting should be done with a sharp knife or professional cutter. Always follow a pattern when cutting.

When molding gum paste, the mold should be lightly dusted first with cornstarch. Then the paste is forced into the mold, removed, and allowed to dry. The drying should be done at room temperature and on a hard, clean surface such as marble or glass. This enables the pieces to dry evenly. When these pieces are half dry, turn them over and allow the other side to dry. When they are completely dry on both sides, sand with a very fine sandpaper for added smoothness.

*Figure A.5   A basket woven with pulled sugar*

Now all the different pieces are ready to be assembled with the aid of additional gum paste that has been thinned down with water or egg white. Gum paste may be colored, but a plain white display piece seems more effective. If it is to be colored, however, only pastel shades should be used. When these sugar pieces are made for display purposes, the structure should be delicate—not too thick or heavy—as this detracts from their beauty.

There are several recipes for making gum paste. One of the most satisfactory, because of its simplicity and excellent results, follows.

*Figure A.6   Gum paste model of the U.S.S.* Nautilus, *used as a centerpiece*

*Figure A.7   Gum paste model of a stagecoach*

## GUM PASTE OR PASTILLAGE

| | | |
|---|---|---|
| Gelatin | | 1 oz |
| Water | | 8 oz (variable) |
| Confectioners' sugar | 5 lb | |

*Method:* Place gelatin in a container of water and heat until it is dissolved. Cool slightly, add the sugar, and mix until smooth. The consistency of the paste should be firm but pliable. Store it in a container until ready to work and roll. It may be stored in a refrigerator for further use.

## NOUGAT CANDY FOR FANCY DISPLAY WORK

Nougat candy, used for display work, is quite simple to make. There are a variety of novelty pieces that may be made from it such as books, baskets, Easter eggs, hats, and so on. If it is possible to watch a demonstration, it will be easier for the beginner. After seeing an experienced worker handle the product, then practice doing it yourself as much as possible.

A marble slab or a hard surface, which should be slightly oiled to prevent sticking, is required for this work. Other tools needed are a heavy rolling pin, spatula, and a French knife, slightly oiled.

When the candy is cooked, pour the mixture on the hard surface, turning the edges of the mixture toward the center until it starts to set. While it is still hot, cut out or mold the nougat into the shapes desired. It must be hot and flexible while handling. After it is cut or molded, allow it to cool and set until firm. If the mixture should cool and become firm while the cutting or molding is taking place, put it in a warm oven until it is flexible again.

For assembling the pieces, use a candy syrup of sugar and water cooked to 312°F. If a decoration of flowers or a special design is desired, royal icing may be used.

## NOUGAT CANDY

| | | |
|---|---|---|
| Sugar | 3 lb | |
| Water (1 pint) | 1 lb | |
| Corn syrup | | 8 oz |
| Almonds, warm, sliced | 3 lb | |
| | 7 lb | 8 oz |

*Method:* Cook sugar, water, and syrup to 320°F. Add almonds and stir.

## THE ROMANTIC HISTORY OF CHOCOLATE

The Western world—meaning Europe—had not even heard of chocolate when Columbus began his explorations in 1492. When he returned from the first voyage of discovery, he laid at the feet of King Ferdinand of Spain a variety

*Figure A.8   Nougat showpieces*

of wonders, including samples of a most unpromising dark brown bean—the cacao bean.

It remained for Hernando Cortés to discover, when a guest in the court of Aztec Emperor Montezuma II in 1519, that this unlikely bean could be made into a beverage. Montezuma served it in large golden goblets and called it "chocolate."

It was too bitter for the Spanish taste when Cortés introduced it at home, but one of his countrymen conceived the idea of sweetening it with cane sugar. Another contemporary Spaniard decided to add cinnamon, a third gave it a dash of vanilla, a fourth thought it would taste better if served hot— and an industry was born. Spaniards started raising cacao beans commercially in their overseas possessions.

For nearly a hundred years, they managed to keep the preparation of chocolate a secret, but Spanish monks finally leaked the secret. The taste of chocolate spread to France and England. Hand methods of manufacture in small shops gave way to mass production. The cocoa press, invented in 1828, improved the flavor and consistency by squeezing out part of the cocoa butter. In 1876, a Swiss named Daniel Peter revolutionized the industry. Experimenting with a milk product produced by his neighbor Nestle, he invented milk chocolate for eating.

Partly as a result of Peter's revolutionary discovery, eating chocolate has far outstripped drinking chocolate in terms of pounds produced. It has become a billion-dollar industry, providing employment for tens of thousands all over the world.

The bean grows on an evergreen tree in shady, moist, tropical ground. The blossoms, waxy pink or white, have a curiously artificial appearance. The pods sprout from the trunk and main branches and are first green or maroon in color. They grow and ripen into an elongated melon shape, colored flecked gold or scarlet.

When the woody pods have been cut from the trees, they are hacked open with machetes and the cream-colored beans are scooped out. After a period of fermentation, the beans are dried and prepared for shipping in large sacks.

At the factory, the art of chocolate-making takes over. After cleaning, the various varieties of beans are roasted in large rotary cylinders, their thin shells are removed, and the remaining nibs are carefully blended. The blended nibs are crushed at the mill, a process that generates sufficient heat to liquefy the cocoa butter and produce what's known as "chocolate liquor," the basis of all chocolate products.

When the cocoa butter is removed, the resulting cake can be pulverized into drinking cocoa. By contrast, eating chocolate is made by adding cocoa butter; and a characteristic chocolate bar would result from the further addition of milk and highly refined sugar. After painstaking emulsification and tempering, the mixture is poured into molds to cool and is packaged; then one of the discoveries of Columbus goes out to delight a twentieth century schoolchild.


## DECORATING WITH CHOCOLATE

### Chocolate Molding or Couverture

Chocolate used for molding is called "couverture" by European pastry chefs. It is manufactured in the United States in 10-lb blocks and can be purchased from any bakery supply house. Hershey's and Stollwerk's sweet chocolate are generally used for couverture.

Chocolate used for molding or dipping should be melted gradually in a warm water bath or chocolate warmer until the temperature reaches approximately 86°F. The temperature is most important; if over- or underheated, the chocolate will turn gray and lose its gloss.

Break sweet chocolate into small pieces, and melt over a hot water bath (water temperature should not exceed 90°F), stirring well until all pieces are melted.

If chocolate is too thick, add melted cocoa butter until the proper running consistency is obtained. In extremely warm weather, a small addition of melted wax will definitely help the chocolate resist the heat: 1 oz of melted wax to 1 lb of chocolate should be sufficient.

Pour about ⅔ of the whole quantity over a marble slab, and work it with a spatula or a scraper until cool. Mix with the remaining third, and melt to 84°–86°F. This process is called tempering.

Always use a wooden spoon or a steel spatula, rather than your hands, to work chocolate, because the temperature of your hands may cause the melted chocolate to discolor.

Chocolate molds are made out of tin or plastic and must always be kept dry and very clean. Scraping the inside of a mold with any sharp instrument will cause the chocolate to stick to the mold, so that future unmolding will be impossible.

## CHOCOLATE DECORATIONS AND GARNISHES

The first step in making chocolate decorations is to cut a large bar of chocolate into small pieces with a French knife. The chocolate is then put into a bowl and melted at about 115°F. While the chocolate is melting, it must be kept free from any contact with water or liquid of any kind as this tends to cause it to stiffen and lose its liquid form. Be careful not to overheat the chocolate or heat it too quickly. Temperatures over 120°F will make the chocolate thick and coarse.

Cool the chocolate to about 85°F; if necessary, "temper" or add some very finely grated chocolate, which will help the chocolate to set faster.

For curls or shavings, pour a small amount of chocolate on a marble slab and spread it with a spatula knife to form a strip about 4 inches wide and ⅛ inch thick. As soon as the chocolate begins to set, cut the shavings or curls with a quick, forward motion of the knife. The chocolate will curl as it comes off the knife in that shape.

For other decorations, let the chocolate cool and set, then cut it into squares or triangles with a knife, or into various shapes with assorted cutters. The chocolate may be stored in a cool, dry place until needed, and then easily be applied to finished pastries, cakes, and desserts. If your first attempt is not successful, nothing is lost. Simply scrap the chocolate back into the heating pot and start over from the beginning.

## Chocolate for Piping or Decorating

Melt sweet chocolate in a cup, and add to it ⅓ of the same amount of fondant icing. Gradually add a little warm syrup or water to make a smooth piping consistency. Use while warm.

## Chocolate Streusel Topping

This topping is widely used for finishing layer cakes and French pastries.

Gradually add a few drops of water to some melted sweet chocolate, and stir continually until chocolate thickens to a rather stiff consistency. Turn a sieve with a medium-sized mesh upside down, and press the chocolate through the sieve. Let the shredded chocolate hang until cool; then separate the shreds from the sieve, and keep in a cool place for future use.

## VARIOUS BAKING TEMPERATURES (APPROXIMATE RANGES)

| | |
|---|---|
| Pan breads | 400°–425°F |
| Pan rolls | 400°F |
| Hearth bread and rolls | 400°–425°F |
| Danish pastry | 375°–400°F |
| Various sweet doughs | 375°–400°F |
| Coffee cake | 375°–400°F |
| Sheet layer cakes | 375°F |
| Angel and sponge cake | 350°–375°F |
| Heavy fruit cake | 325°–350°F |
| Fruit and soft pies | 375°F, 400°F, 425°F |
| Various cookies | 350°–375°F |
| Puffs and éclairs | 375°–400°F |
| Various muffins | 400°–425°F |
| Puff pastes | 350°–375°F |
| Baked puddings | 350°–375°F |

# CONVERSION

# TABLES

## BRITISH MEASURE OF CAPACITY

| | | |
|---|---|---|
| 1 British or Imperial gill | 0.142 liter | |
| 1 British or Imperial pint | 4 gills | 0.568 liters |
| 1 British or Imperial quart | 2 pints | 1.136 liters |
| 1 British or Imperial gallon | 4 Imperial quarts | 4.544 liters |
| 1 British or Imperial barrel | 36 Imperial gallons | |

## UNITED STATES MEASURE OF CAPACITY

| | | |
|---|---|---|
| 1 United States liquid gill | 0.118 liter | |
| 1 United States liquid pint | 4 gills | 0.473 liter |
| 1 United States liquid quart | 2 pints | 0.946 liter |
| 1 United States liquid gallon | 8 pints | 3.785 liters |
| 1 United States barrel | 31½ gallons | 119 liters |

## AVOIRDUPOIS WEIGHT

| | | |
|---|---|---|
| 1 grain | 0.0648 gram | |
| 1 dram | 27.34 grains | 1.77 grams |
| 1 ounce | 16 drams | 28.35 grams |
| 1 pound | 16 ounces | 453.59 grams |
| 1 quarter | 28 pounds | 12.7 kilograms |
| U.S.A. 25 pounds | | 11.34 kilograms |
| 1 butcher's stone | 8 pounds | 6.35 kilograms |
| 1 hundredweight | 4 quarters (112 pounds) | 50.8 kilograms |

## MEASURES OF CAPACITY

| | |
|---|---|
| 1 liter | 10 deciliters |
| | 1.7607 pints |
| | 7.0431 gills |
| | 0.8804 quart |
| | 0.2201 gallon |
| 1 hectoliter | 0.1 liter |
| | 22,009 gallons |
| | 2.751 bushels |

# BAKERS'
# DICTIONARY

Ash: The powdery, incombustible residue left after burning matter.

Average flour value: Value composed of four factors: color of flour, loaves per barrel, size of loaf, and quality of bread as applied to any given shipment of flour.

Baba au rhum: French sweet-dough cake soaked with rum.

Bacteria: Numerous microscopic organisms, various species of which are concerned in fermentation and spoilage.

Bain marie: A double boiler, or open vessel, which has a loose bottom for the reception of hot water, and is used to keep sauces at boiling point.

Bake: To cook by dry heat in a closed place, as an oven.

Baked Alaska: Cake layer topped with firm ice cream, completely covered with meringue, then delicately browned in a very hot oven.

Baking or bicarbonate of soda: A sodium salt of carbonic acid having the ability to combine with acid to produce carbon dioxide. It is alkaline in nature.

Baking powder: A chemical leavening agent composed of baking soda, dry acid, and, usually, cornstarch to absorb air moisture; when wet, carbon dioxide (a gas) is given off to raise the batter.

Barrel: A flat-ended, wooden, somewhat cylindrical container with bulging sides. The measure of what a standard size barrel contains, as $31\frac{1}{2}$ gallons of liquid or 196 lb of flour.

Bars: Cookies made in oblong shapes.

Batter: A pourable mixture of combined ingredients such as flour, sugar, eggs, shortening, milk, etc.

Biscuit: Small roll made with yeast dough. Small round bread stuff made of dough raised with baking powder. Kind of crisp or hard bread, thin and flat, made without leavening.

Biscuit tortoni: Mousse, containing and sprinkled with macaroon crumbs, frozen in individual paper cases.

Blanch: To remove the skins from various nuts, etc., by scalding.

Blancmange: Molded white pudding of milk, sugar, and cornstarch or gelatin.

Bleeding: Term applied to dough that has been cut and left unsealed at the cut, thus permitting the escape of air and gas.

Blend: A mixture of two or more flavorings or grades of flour.

Boil: To bubble, emitting vapor, when heat is applied. Boiling temperature for water is considered as 212°F at ordinary altitudes, but varies with other liquids and other altitudes.

Boiled icing: Made by boiling sugar and water to thread stage (238°F), then adding it to beaten egg whites and confectioners' sugar.

Bolting: Sifting of ground grain to remove the bran.

Boston brown bread: A dark, sweet bread (not yeast raised) containing among the ingredients cornmeal and molasses, steamed and not baked.

Boston cream pie: Plain or sponge cake layers filled with cream filling, often topped with confectioners' sugar or thin chocolate frosting.

Bouchées: Very small puff paste patties, small enough to be a mouthful only.

Bowl knife: A spatula or flexible, dull-edged knife used to scrape batter or dough from bowl sides.

Bran: Skin or outer covering of the wheat berry removed during milling.

Bran muffin: Sweet muffin containing a large percentage of bran.

Brandy: An alcoholic liquor distilled from fermented fruit juice or wine.

Bread: The accepted term for food of flour, sugar, shortening, salt, and liquid made light by the action of yeast.

Bread dough: The uncooked mass of ingredients used to make bread.

Bread faults: Deviations from standards of perfection, used to determine wrong factors in the process of production of bread.

Bread schedule: List of exact periods of dough fermentation; also shows time needed for completing the baking process.

Bread scoring: Analysis of finished loaf to determine quality.

Bread shop order: Form sent to shop foreman giving amount of bread needed for production during, or by, a given time.

Brioche: A light sweet dough, baked in large or small molds.

Buns: Small cakes of bread dough, sometimes slightly sweetened or flavored.

Butter: Fat obtained by churning sweet or sour cream.

Butter cream frosting: Rich, uncooked frosting containing powdered sugar, butter and/or other shortening, and egg white.

Butter horns: Basic sweet dough cut and shaped like horns.

Butter sponge: Sponge cake batter, to which shortening is added. Used for torten and French pastry, also some layers.

Butter stars: Cookies made by pressing rich dough through star tube.

Butterscotch: A flavor produced by the use of butter and brown sugar.

Cacao: An evergreen tree, native to tropical America, from which chocolate is obtained.

Cake: A leavened and shortened sweet product containing flour, sugar, salt, egg, milk, liquid, flavoring, shortening, and leavening agent.

Cake faults: Deviations from standards of perfection for the type.

Cake machine: Machine with vertical agitators operating at different speeds, used for mixing cake ingredients.

Cane sugar: A sweet carbohydrate obtained from sugar cane.

Caramel buns: Sweet-dough pieces baked in a sugared pan.

Caramel icing: Cooked icing of brown sugar, shortening, and milk.

Caramel sugar: Cane sugar boiled to a certain density, then cooled and pulled for use in decorating.

Caramelized sugar: Dry sugar heated, with constant stirring, until it melts and darkens in color; used for flavoring and color.

Caraway seeds: Aromatic seeds, tiny and egg-shaped. Used in sauerkraut, cookies, cheese, German rye bread.

Carbohydrates: Sugars and starches derived chiefly from vegetable sources, which contained set amounts of carbon, hydrogen, and oxygen according to the kind of carbohydrate.

Carbon dioxide: A colorless, tasteless, edible gas obtained during fermentation or from the combination of soda and acid.

Carbonated ammonia: Leavening agent made of ammonia and carbonic acid.

Cardamom: Angular, aromatic seeds of herb grown in India and Ceylon, and having aniselike taste. Used whole or ground in pickling, breads, cookies, and many Scandinavian desserts.

Casein: The principal nitrogenous, or protein, part of milk.

Chafing dish: A dish (usually silver) set within another dish containing hot water, with a small lamp underneath, and used for keeping foods hot until served.

Charlotte: Mold lined with ladyfingers and filled with fruit and whipped cream. **Russe:** Mold lined with ladyfingers and filled with Bavarian cream.

Cheese cake: Cake made of sweet or short dough base with a filling of cheese combined with eggs and milk.

Cheese torte: A rich cheese mixture baked in a shell of combined crumbs, sugar, and butter.

Cherries jubilee: Cherries set aflame with kirsch or brandy. Often served over vanilla ice cream.

Chinois: A cone-shaped strainer also used for pureeing foods.

Chocolate snaps: Fairly crisp drop cookies flavored with chocolate.

Cinnamon: The aromatic bark of certain trees of the laurel family; ground and used as a spice flavoring.

Citron: The sweetened rind of a fruit.

Clear flour: Flour made from middlings after patent flour is taken.

Cobbler: Sweetened fruit in deep dish, topped with upper crust and baked.

Cocoa: A powder made from chocolate minus most of its cocoa butter.

Coconut: The inside meat of the coconut, shredded or grated.

Coffee cake: Sweet bread in various shapes, with filling and topping.

Colors: Shades produced by using vegetable dyes; flour colors.

Compote: Fruit stewed in syrup, or a mixture of different stewed fruits.

Compounds: In the baking industry, certain mixtures of fats and oils.

Congealing point: Temperature at which liquid becomes solid.

Corn flour: Coarse flour ground from corn; finer than meal.

Corn muffin: Sweet muffin containing corn flour or meal.

Cornet: A cornucopia-shaped (horn-shaped) container of paper or cloth used for tubing soft doughs, frostings, etc.

Cornmeal: Granular form of corn somewhat coarser than corn flour.

Cottage cheese: The drained curd of soured cow's milk.

Coupe: A dessert served in a champagne glass, and usually made of fresh fruit and ice cream.

Cream: The fat part of cow's milk; a thickened, cooked mass of sugar, egg, milk, and a thickener; used for pies and fillings.

Cream cheese: The drained curd of soured cream, pressed.

Cream pies: One-crust pies having cream filling, topped with whipped cream or meringue.

Cream puffs: Baked puffs of cream puff dough (pâte à chou) that are hollow; usually filled with whipped cream or a cream filling.

Cream rolls: Puff paste rolled and baked in spiral shape, then filled with whipped cream or marshmallow.

Creaming: The process of beating sugar and shortening.

Crème: Cream or cream sauce.

Crème Chantilly: Cream whipped with vanilla and sugar.

Crème de menthe: A green flavoring of light mint taste.

Crepes: Very thin pancakes. **Suzette:** Pancakes served in butter sauce flavored with orange, lemon, curaçao; flamed in brandy.

Crescent rolls: Hard-crusted rolls shaped into crescents, often with seeds on top.

Croissant: Rich crescent-shaped French roll usually served at breakfast.

Crullers: Long, twisted baking powder doughnuts.

Culinary: This word is applied to anything connected with the art of cooking or baking.

Cupcakes: Small cakes of layer cake batter baked in muffin pans.

Currant: The acidulous berry of a shrub; usually used dried.

Custard: A sweetened mixture of eggs and milk that is baked or cooked over hot water.

Danish pastry: A flaky yeast dough having butter rolled into it and filled with almond, cheese, jam, or other filling.

Date: The fruit of a species of palm, very sweet.

Date filling: A cooked blend of dates, water, and sugar.

Decoration: Trimming with fancy designs or ornamentation.

Detection of flour: The manner in which poor flour is contrasted with a good flour to show that the former has been bleached.

Determination of ash: The finding of the ash content of flour.

Determination of flour color: Comparison of flour samples to show how they approach color standards.

Dextrin: A soluble, gummy substance formed from starch by the action of heat, ferments, etc., having characteristic properties.

Dextrose: Sugar of vegetables (except beet) less sweet than cane or beet sugar and simpler in structure, chemically speaking.

Diastase: An enzyme possessing the power to convert starches into dextrin and maltose (a simple sugar).

Dissolve: To liquefy or carry in suspension in liquid.

Divider: A machine to cut dough automatically into a required size.

Dough: The thick, uncooked mass of combined ingredients for bread, rolls, cookies, etc.; usually applied to bread.

Dough room: Special room in which bread doughs are mixed.

Dough room record: A sheet of paper showing the time and losses of dough going through different stages (bread dough).

Dough sheet: A paper showing the formulas for a day's doughs.

Dough temperature: Temperature of dough at different stages.

Dough time cards: Cards usually punched with a time clock at different stages of dough processing.

Doughnut: A round cake, usually with center hole, made of yeast or baking powder dough and cooked in hot deep fat.

Doughnut kettle: A large kettle used for frying doughnuts.

Doughnut screens: Screens used to lift doughnuts from fat or for keeping them under the fat surface during cooking.

Doughnut sticks: Wooden sticks for turning doughnuts while cooking.

Drops: Small globules of liquid that will drip instead of flow from spoon or container; a form of cookie.

Dry fruit: Fruit from which moisture has been removed by drying.

Dry milk: Milk from which water has been removed by drying.

Dry yeast: A dehydrated form of yeast.

Dusting: Distributing a film of flour on pans or work bench.

Dusting flour: Flour spread on work bench to prevent sticking.


Éclair: A long, thin shell of the same paste as cream puffs.

Egg wash: A mixture of eggs and water (or milk) in equal parts applied to an unbaked product by brush to produce a glazed effect and to give the product a rich brown color.

Emulsify: To combine ingredients together such as water and fat.

English brandy snaps: Spicy cookies, very small and flat.

Enriched bread: Bread made from enriched flour or containing federally prescribed amounts of thiamin, riboflavin, iron, and niacin.

Enzyme: A minute substance produced by living organisms, which has the power to bring about changes in organic materials.

Evaporated milk: Unsweetened canned milk from which water has been removed before canning.

Expansion of dough: The stage of dough production where the most air has been assimilated.

Extract: Essence of fruits or spices used as flavoring.


Ferment: A substance, such as yeast, producing fermentation.

Fermentation: The chemical changes of an organic compound due to action of living organisms, such as yeast, producing the formation of the leavening gas, carbon dioxide.

Fig: A pear-shaped fruit of the fig tree.

Filberts: Cultivated hazelnuts.

Filbert rolls: Jelly roll type of cake with roasted filberts in filling and batter.

Fillings: Sweet creams, jams, etc., between baked layers, in cake rolls, or shaped into yeast-raised goods.

Finger roll: A bun about 3 inches long and 1 inch wide.

Firing: Process of heating an oven with fuel.

Flambé: Dessert over which spirits are poured and lighted.

Flavor: An extract, emulsion, or spice used to produce a pleasant taste. The taste of a finished product.

Fleurons: Garnitures made from light puff paste cut into oval, diamond, or crescent shapes, and served with meat, fish, or soup.

Flour: Finely ground meal of grain (wheat, rye, etc.).

Flour scales: Large platform scales used to show weight of flour when delivered and when used, to detect losses by shrinkage.

Fluff: A mass of beaten egg white and crushed fruit.

Foam: Mass of beaten egg and sugar, as in sponge cake, before adding flour.

Fold: The method of lapping dough over on itself after it reaches right fermentation, as in making yeast-raised sweet goods.

Fondant: An icing of boiled sugar and water, without egg white.

Fondant slab: Marble slab on which fondant is worked until creamy.

Formula: In baking, a recipe giving ingredients, amounts to be used, and method of combining them.

Foundation: The reinforced base on which an oven or machine rests.

French bread: An unsweetened crusty bread baked in a narrow strip and containing very little shortening.

French doughnuts: Doughnuts made of pâte à chou.

French knife: A long knife with pointed blade used in cutting cakes, doughs, and nuts.

Fritters: Doughnuts made from cream puff paste and fried in hot deep fat. Fruit-filled drops of heavy cake batter fried in deep fat.

Fruit cake: A cake containing large amounts of dried fruits and nuts with only enough batter to bind the fruit together.

Frying: In the baking industry, cooking in hot deep fat.

Fuel: Anything which is burned to give heat.

Garnishing bag: Similar to a cornet and equipped with fancy tips.

Gateau: French term for cake.

Gelatinization of starch: Formation of jellylike substance when moistened starch is cooked.

Germ: That part of seed (such as in grain) from which the new plant grows.

Ginger: The spicy root of a tropical plant used for flavoring.

Glacé: Sugar treated so as to look like ice.

Gliadin: The part of gluten that gives it elasticity.

Glucose: A simple sugar made by action of acid on starch (corn syrup).

Gluten: The protein part of flour that gives structure to bakery products by enabling flour to expand around air or gas and to hold the texture so formed. The determining quality factor.

Glutenin: The part of gluten that gives it strength.

Gourmet: A connoisseur of fine foods.

Grading: Separating middlings of wheat according to size.

Graham flour: Unbolted wheat meal.

Graham muffin: A sweet muffin with graham flour as its main ingredient.

Greasing: Spreading a film of fat on a surface.

Gum arabic: A gum obtained from a species of acacia tree.

Gum paste: A white modeling substance of gum tragacanth or gelatin, water, and sugar.

Gum tragacanth: A gum used to give firmness.

Hamburger roll: A soft, round bun about 4 inches in diameter.

Hardness of water: An indication of mineral salts in greater amount than is found in soft water.

Hazelnut: Nut of a wild American shrub, smaller than the filbert.

Hearth: The heated baking surface or floor of an oven.

Holland rusk: Toast of yeast biscuits rich in milk, eggs, etc.

Homemade bread: Plain topped bread rolled in flour before panning, or that baked in household-type bread pans.

Honey: A sweet syrup substance made by bees from flower nectar.

Horn of plenty: Cornucopia-shaped cookie made with gum paste, butter cream trimming, or bread dough.

Horseshoes: Danish or puff pastry shaped like horseshoes.

Hot-cross buns: Sweet, yeast-raised buns with raisins added, marked on top with a cross in dough or a frosted cross. Lenten favorite.

Humidity: Amount of moisture in the air.

Hydrogenated oil: Oil treated with hydrogen to give a type of shortening.

Hygrometer: An instrument to determine the degree of humidity.

Ice: To frost or put on an icing or frosting; frozen water.

Icing: A frosting or coating for cakes made by mixing confectioners' sugar with water, egg whites, etc.

Infection: The presence of injurious microorganisms.

Ingredients: Food materials blended to give palatable products.

Inventory: Itemized list of goods and equipment on hand, together with the estimated worth or cost.

Invert sugar: A simple sugar; combination of dextrose and levulose.

Jelly: A stiffened combination of fruit juice and sugar, stiffened by the action of the sugar on the pectin in the fruit.

Jelly wreath: A rolled ring of basic sweet dough containing jelly.

Kernel paste: A mass of ground apricot kernels and sugar.

Kisses: A meringue confection of egg white and sugar baked slowly.

Lactose: The sugar of cow's milk.

Lady Baltimore cake: Rich white layer cake with fruit and nut filling and white icing.

Lard: Rendered hog fat.

Leavening: Raising or lightening by air, steam, or gas (carbon dioxide).

Leavening agent: An ingredient (or ingredients) used to introduce carbon dioxide: yeast, baking powder, or soda plus sour milk.

Leipziger stollen: Very rich coffee cake with a great deal of fruit.

Levulose: A simple sugar found in honey and fruits.

Liason: A mixture of egg yolks and cream used to thicken and enrich sauces.

Line: To place paste, pie crust, ladyfingers, etc., around the inside edge or bottom of molds, rings, plates.

Linzer torte: A heavy cake of macaroon paste and jelly.

Loaf bread: Bread baked in pans.

Loaf cake: Cake baked in a bread pan or similar deep container.

Macaroon paste: A combination of almond and kernel paste.

Macaroons: Small cookies of nut paste (as almond), sugar, and egg white.

Make up: Method of mixing ingredients or handling of dough.

Malt extract: A syrupy liquid obtained from malt mash.

Maple flavoring: An extract of maple sugar or a syrup so flavored.

Maraschino: Cordial distilled from marasca cherry juice.

Maraschino cherries: Artificially colored white cherries in maraschino.

Marble cake: Cake of two or three colored batters partially mixed.

Marrons: Chestnuts. **Glacés:** Chestnuts preserved in syrup or candied, used in making fancy desserts.

Marshmallow: A white confection of meringuelike consistency.

Marzipan: Almond paste used for modeling, masking, and torten.

Masking: Act of covering with icing or frosting or such.

Meal: Coarsely ground grain; unbolted wheat flour.

Measuring: Apportioning ingredients by area, volume, or weight. Ascertaining dimensions, capacities, or weight.

Measuring cup: A standardized cup marked with fractions of a cup, used for accurate measure.

Measuring spoons: Sets of standardized spoons (tablespoon, teaspoon, half, and quarter) ensuring accurate measurement.

Melba sauce: Raspberry and currant jelly made into a sauce.

Melba toast: Thin slices of bread toasted to a pleasing crispness and golden color.

Melting point: The temperature at which a solid becomes liquid.

Meringue: A white frothy mass of beaten egg white and sugar.

Metric system: A system of weights and measures based on multiple units of 10; used in the baking industry chiefly for flour analysis.

Middlings: Coarse particles of ground wheat made during rolling of the grain in flour mills.

Milk bread: White bread in which all liquid is milk or which contains not less than 8.8 parts (by weight) of milk solids for each 100 parts of flour (by weight). This is a federal standard that is rigidly enforced.

Milk solids: All of cow's milk except the water.

Mincemeat: Combination filling of fruit, spices, beef, and suet.

Mix: The combined ingredients of a batter or dough.

Mixing: The blending of ingredients.

Mixing bowl: A concave, hemispherical container for mixing.

Mocha: A flavor combination of coffee and cocoa.

Moisture: Water held in or appearing on a substance.

Molasses: Light to dark brown syrup obtained in making cane sugar.

Mold infection: Deleterious microscopic organisms of vegetable nature.

Molder: Machine that shapes dough pieces for various shapes.

Mousse: A light, frozen dessert consisting of whipped cream, pâte à bombe, and flavoring.

Muffins: Small, light quickbread baked in muffin pans.

Mushrooms: Schaum torte confections in mushroom shapes.

Napoleons: Delicate French pastry made with puff paste in layers with a cream filling between and thin frosting or powdered sugar on top.

Nappe: To coat with sauce; thicken.

Neapolitan ice cream: Layered brick ice cream in different flavors.

Nesselrode pie: Rum-flavored Bavarian cream pie filling with mixed preserved fruits and chestnuts added in a flaky pie shell and topped with shaved chocolate.

Nougat: A confection made from almonds, pistachio nuts, and sugar.

Oatmeal: Meal made by grinding oats.

One mix: A cake-mixing method where all ingredients are combined and beaten at one time.

Pandowdy: Sweetened and spiced sliced apples covered with a rich baking powder biscuit dough, then baked. Served hot with cream.

Pans (tins): Variously shaped metal containers for cooking and baking.

Parker House rolls: Folded buns of fairly rich dough.

Pastillage: A gum paste used in making candies, fancy pieces, flowers, etc.

Pâte à chou: Paste used in making éclairs, cream puffs, French doughnuts, etc.

Patent flour: The fine meal of ground spring wheat.

Pectin: A natural fruit substance that, when in right balance with sugar and acid, forms fruit juice into a jelly.

Petit fours: Small cakes of various shapes and flavors.

Pfeffernuss: Christmas cookie, spicy and hard.

Philadelphia cinnamon bun: Raisin-filled cinnamon bun with luscious sticky topping.

Pie: Dessert with pastry bottom, fruit or cream filling, and meringue, whipped cream, or pastry top.

Pignoli: Pine nuts.

Pine nuts: Small, sweet seeds contained in cones of certain pine trees, usually roasted or salted.

Plain tube decorating: Decorations made with plain round tube.

Poppy seeds: Fragrant seeds from Holland, used in breads, rolls, noodles, etc.

Profiteroles: Small cream puffs filled with cream and covered with a sauce. They are sometimes made very small and served with soup.

Proof box: Box or cabinet equipped with shelves; it also permits the introduction of heat and steam; used for fermenting dough.

Proofing period: The time during which dough rises.

Puff paste: Rich pastry with rolled butter and special shortening for added flakiness.

Pumpernickel: Coarse, somewhat acid rye bread.

Pumpernickel meal: Coarse rye flour.

Punch: See **Fold**.

Quiche lorraine: Open-faced cheese pie with diced ham or bacon added.

Quick bread: Dough for bread or rolls raised by baking powder.

Raisins: Dried sweet grapes, either dark or bleached.

Rock sugar: A candy preparation used in the construction of fancy pieces.

Rocks: Small, rough-surfaced cookies resembling stone shapes.

Rolling pin: Smooth-surfaced wooden piece for rolling dough.

Rolls: Soft breads sometimes called buns; hard-crusted pieces of lean dough.

Rope: A spoiling bacterial growth in bread formed during production.

Rounding: Shaping of dough pieces to seal ends and prevent bleeding.

Royal icing: Decorative frosting of cooked sugar and egg whites.


Sabayon: Pudding sauce, made in double boiler, of eggs, sugar, and wine. Served hot.

Sally Lunn: Southern bread sometimes yeast-leavened and baked in tube pan. Or it may be made with baking powder and baked in round cake or pie pans.

Salt: Sodium chloride; used for flavor and dough control.

Saturation: Absorption to the limit of capacity.

Scale: An instrument for weighing.

Scaling: Apportioning batter or dough according to unit weight.

Schaum torte: A torte made with a baked meringue and whipped cream.

Schedule: Shop form designating amount and types of goods to be made and hour when needed.

Scone: Typical Scottish hot bread or cake baked on a griddle or in the oven.

Score: To score is to make incisions forming a pattern on cakes or pies, etc.

Scoring: Judging finished goods according to points of favor.

Sesame seed: Seed imported from Asia. Creamy white, tiny, somewhat slippery to touch, with faint nutty odor and nutlike flavor. Nice in breads, cookies, etc.

Shoofly pie: Brown sugar and molasses-flavored cake, baked in a pie shell.

Short pastry: A dough made with a high fat content, such as pie crust.

Shortbread: Crisp cookie, rich in butter or other shortening, of Scottish origin.

Shortening: Fat or oil used to tenderize flour products.

Shrink: To roll out paste and allow it to rest before baking in order to prevent shrinkage.

Sifting: Passing through fine sieve for perfect blending and to remove foreign or oversize particles.

Snaps: Small cookies that run flat during baking.

Solidifying point: Temperature at which a fluid changes to a solid.

Soufflé: Baked dish made basically of milk and eggs, to which the beaten egg whites, folded in last, give a high, puffed, airy lightness; may be main dish or dessert.

Spices: Aromatic vegetable substances (dry) for flavoring.

Spoon bread: Southern corn bread made in a casserole, so delicate it must be served with a spoon.

Springerle: Traditional German cookie, anise-flavored, with a raised design on top.

Stollen: Raisin-filled rich yeast bread.

Straight flour: Flour containing all of the wheat berry except the bran and feeds; termed 100% extraction flour.

Strawberries Romanoff: Fine, ripe strawberries marinated in Cointreau or kirsch, with whipped cream folded in or used as topping.

Strudel: Rich pastry filled with apples, cherries, plums, etc.

Tarts: Pastries with heavy fruit or cream filling.

Tea rolls: Small sweet buns.

Temperature: Degree of heat or cold.

Tempering: Adjusting temperature of ingredients to a certain degree.

Testing: Trying a cake or bread at the oven for doneness; checking product or ingredients for quality, according to a set method.

Texture: Interior grain or structure of a baked product as shown by a cut surface; the feeling of a substance under the fingers.

Thermometer: An instrument for measuring temperature.

Torten: Large fancy cakes enriched with creams, marzipan, etc.

Trifle: Dessert of English origin made of layers of wine-sprinkled sponge cake slices, custard sauce or whipped cream, and preserves or jelly.

Troughs: Large, rather shallow containers, usually on wheels, used for holding large masses of rising dough.

Tubing: Pressing a substance through a decorating or other tube.

Turn: When puff paste is mixed, rolled out, folded over one third, and then the other third is folded over this, this operation is called giving one turn.

Tutti-frutti: A confection or filling made of a fruit mixture.

Vanilla bean: Dried bean of a tropical orchid, used for flavoring. Extract is delightful in desserts, cakes, cookies, etc.

Vegetable colors: Vegetable liquids or paste, used for coloring.

Vienna bread: A hearth bread with heavy, crisp crust, sometimes finished with a seed topping.

Vol-au-vent: A light puff paste, cut either round or oval, and usually filled with meat or fish.

Wash: A liquid brushed on the surface of an unbaked product (may be water, milk, starch solution, thin syrup, or egg).

Washington pie: Sponge cake layers filled with jelly, sprinkled on top with confectioners' sugar.

Whip: To beat to a froth; an instrument consisting of strong wires held together by a handle and used for whipping.

Whole wheat: Unbolted wheat meal.

Yeast: A microscopic fungus (plant) that reproduces by budding and causes fermentation and the giving off of carbon dioxide.

Zwieback: A toast made of rich coffee cake.

# INDEX